MW00324194

Wellspring of Words

Contact Information
Dr. Denise Williams
coachorcounselor@gmail.com

All Scripture quotations, unless otherwise indicated, are taken from *The Scofield Study Bible. Holy Bible, King James Version. KJV.* Copyright 1909, 1917; copyright renewed 1937, 1945 by Oxford University Press, Inc.

Copyright © 2020
All rights reserved. No portion of this book may be reproduced, stored in a retrieval system, or transmitted in any form or by any means: electronic, mechanical, photocopy, recording, or any other, except for brief quotation in printed reviews, without the prior written permission from the author.

Transformed Life Publications Clermont Florida USA
wcsolomon@aol.com
Printed in the USA

This work is dedicated to:
Mavis and Joscelyn Williams
and
Ena Lois Cameron

Whose courage and legacy lives on in
Donna, Naydene, Mark, Peter
Adrienne, Alexandra, Arielle, and Ashley

Table of Contents

Introduction

"Pleasant words are as an honeycomb, sweet to the soul, and health to the bones." Proverbs 16:24

The scriptures declare that "pleasant words are as an honeycomb, sweet to the soul, and health to the bones". When I first read these words, I was mesmerized. For some reason, I was surprised and pleased that the scriptures from thousands of years ago, was stating something that science has fairly recently confirmed. The thought that pleasant words do bring us joy and health, suggests that when we choose to use words that are kind, gentle, considerate, gracious, good-natured, tender, thoughtful, warm, and in other ways pleasing, we feed our souls, we nourish our minds, we attract good health, and add quality years to our lives.

This verse also suggests that this outcome is true whether we speak pleasant words to ourselves with our thoughts, or to others. After all, we may use our words to communicate or express thoughts, ideas, emotions, knowledge or other types of information to others... and to ourselves.

This verse got my mind going as I considered and meditated on it. Over time, two main questions kept returning to me:

1) How is it possible that pleasant words can give us good health and joy?

2) How can I develop a habit of consistently choosing words that bestow good health and impart life?

My search for answers to these questions, led me to the lessons, observations, insights, and necessary actions that I will share throughout the pages of this book.

When I decided to conduct this research, I started to notice the affinity we humans tend to have for dousing our dreams, our ideas, our plans, and even our hopes, with doubts and negative words. My sister calls those people, 'dream killers'. For example, you may have an idea to do something grand, seek out a new destination, pursue an interest, or create a work of art. The idea might not be fully baked, and yet, in your mind, you can imagine the successful end of your dream. So, you begin to vibrate... then bubble with excitement. You cannot wait to share it with that one person who will help your idea soar on the wings of their encouragement, because all you will really need to propel you forward is for someone to tell you, "yes, you can do it". So, you share your idea, and your excitement, and then 'splaaaaat'! They kill your joy with words like, "*I don't think that's a good idea*", or "*you can't do thaaaat!*" It does not matter what they try to say after they notice the excitement draining from your face, or the enthusiasm vanishing from your voice. Also, you are often not able to erase the impact of those initial words that tried to squeeze out the life from your idea. Instead of saying, "*you've got this,*" or "*I believe you can do this*", or other words to cheer you on, they spread their doubts and fears onto your hopes and dreams, and you've just let them.

They have thrown water on the passionate flame of your ideas. In that moment, quite possibly, they are seeing your ability, your determination, or your motivation, through the lens of their own bias or their own fear. Who are these people? Are they the ambassadors of doubt or skepticism that we have accepted into our lives? Are these the naysayers or dream killers who have convinced us that only they know what is best for us and only they can see clearly what lies ahead for us? Here's a thought, I believe many of them may actually want the very best for us, although it is hard to tell from the words they use.

Yet it's not only 'they' who talk us out of our aspirations. We also kill our own dreams. We spoil our own hopes and dampen our own joy. Maybe something happened in our lives, maybe someone said or did

3

something terrible to us. It could be that we were abandoned, abused, betrayed, bullied, discarded, or otherwise mistreated. Maybe someone hurt us and left us feeling inadequate, defective, or questioning our self-worth. Whatever the cause, we developed a narrative that slithers in and out of our consciousness, like an insidious recording on auto replay, "I'm not good enough", "I'm not pretty, or thin, or fat, or smart, or rich, or [fill in with the word you have used ---------] enough", "I'm not as good as those others", "I can't do *thaaat*".

On another hand, how often do we hold onto some terrible event that happened or that was said to us? How many times do we form a negative narrative in our head because the dream did not turn out the way we had hoped? When that happens, do we tell ourselves we are a failure, do we feel embarrassed, or do we imagine that we have fallen well below some impossible standard? If so, we are likely to feel exposed, vulnerable, and mortified, then we are likely to re-start the cycle of critical self judgements.

If this is your pattern, it does not have to be this way. I believe we have all listened to a narrative that is born of doubt, deficiency, fear, faults, and failings, at one time or other. Many of us have even embraced and over-identified with this narrative.

4

In 2007, when a junior Senator from Illinois announced he would be running for the office of the presidency, many people said, he should not run, he would not win, he did not have enough experience. Senator Obama's campaign kept repeating the words, "*Yes you can, yes we can*". In 2008, Senator Barack Obama won the Presidential election and went on to become the 44th President of the United States, because he believed he could. Regardless of whether or not you and I admired or voted for him, he served that office for two consecutive terms, which was a total of eight years.

There are many words that people speak that can douse our dreams and cause our spirit to plunge. Words like those of the college professor who told my friend Lisa she could not write. Lisa has since earned a doctorate; she owns her business and is also a published author. Words like those of my graduate school professor who told me I would never get the job as a Consultant, because I was too much of an introvert. Upon graduation, I was immediately hired by a top 5 global, consulting firm.

Words like those of people in the administration, who told my pastor, he would NEVER get into medical school. My Pastor is a licensed physician who has been providing medical care for more than 30 years. Dr. Bonaparte operates a health clinic, where he and his staff provide free medical services to the underserved. Words that cause us to feel silenced as though no one would want to hear what we have to say. Words that cause a young girl to think she will not amount to anything, or make a young boy think it would be hopeless to try because his dreams are beyond his reach. These and other pernicious words, spoken by people who we believe have authority about our lives or our future, are bitter and harmful to our health and our purpose. They serve to discourage and can rob us of our hopes and dreams, unless something changes.

Yet we do not ever have to accept the words of doubters when God's Word says we have power to get through difficult situations (Luke 10:19). We have the ability to push away disbelief because God's Word tells us we are more than conquerors (Romans 8:37). God's Word tells us we are overcomers and we are victorious (1 John 5:4-5). God's Word tells us, we can do all things through Christ who gives us strength (Philippians 4:13). God's Word tells us, we are fully capable and competent (2 Corinthians 3:5), and that He who has begun a good work will carry it to completion (Philippians 1:6). God's Word tells us we do not have to be fearful because He will be with us (Isaiah 41:10), He wants the best for us (Jeremiah 29:11), He will not withhold any good thing from us (Psalm 84:11), and He will fight for us (Exodus 14:14), always.

6

We use words to interact and communicate with others. We use words when we pray to our Father in Heaven. When we communicate to ourselves – whether by thoughts and ideas, or by the written or spoken language, most of us are using words and these words have force. They have power. There are many words that can lift our spirits and propel us toward our personal greatness. There are words that remind us to live and to hope. There are words that we can use to bring sweetness to our soul and health to our bones. These words are invigorating and wholesome. Let's use these words.

This work embodies some of the lessons I have learned from the stories of others, and the result of several well-placed seeds that have been sown over the course of my life, that have helped me to open my heart and my mind to respect the authority that is in the words we speak and the thoughts we form. Words and thoughts ferment into beliefs that affect the ways we hold ourselves, walk in our lives, and lead us either to thrive and live the best life that God intended for us, or to barely survive as we are infested with hurtful, ruinous words. I have watched how seeds of just the right words that were sown into the lives of others, whose stories are documented in history books, or passed down by oral traditions throughout generations; have manifested themselves in a powerful life, while other seeds yield the prophecy of a diminished life.

7

Section I

A wellspring, according to the Merriam-Webster and other dictionaries, refers to a source or a plentiful supply of something. From the moment we start to learn language and words, we begin to accumulate our own wellspring of words.

There are words we use automatically, over and over, without consciously realizing the impact they have. We draw from the wellspring at our convenience and we add to it almost daily. Yet, have you ever considered the quality of your wellspring? Have you ever stopped to ask yourself, *"Does the supply of words that I use, build me up or break me down?"*

The following chapters will help you to answer for yourself, how healthy is your Wellspring of Words?

Chapter 1

Set Clear Intentions

"Let the words of my mouth, and the meditation of my heart, be acceptable in thy sight, O LORD, my strength, and my redeemer." Psalm 19:14

The unfathomable power of words lies somewhere amidst the beauty, the charm, and a certain mystery that is sometimes difficult to pinpoint or to miss. Carefully knit and well-chosen words can bring things to life in ways that are compelling. I listen keenly, as people use words to tell intriguing, persuasive, and fascinating stories. I also believe that we have the ability to teach, to entertain, to encourage, to inspire, to influence, and to bless others with our words. However, regrettably, it has become increasingly evident that we also use our words in ways that judge, condemn, criticize, disparage, curse, and in other ways hurt others and ourselves; even when these very words hold us back from the life we deserve to live.

God's Word has already told us that **WE** are God's workmanship created to produce good works (Ephesians 2:10); that we are fearfully and wonderfully made (Psalm 139:14); and that after God created us, He saw that His creation was very good (Genesis 1:31). This means that we ought to acknowledge who we are, and we ought to make every effort to honor this intricately, wonderful creation – God's workmanship, with words and thoughts that are befitting. This also means that we might aim to live our lives, fueled by words that will steer us toward a goal of good works, in whatever shape those works manifest.

Each one of us – God's workmanship, has been designed to produce good works. We are called to be productive and to use the precious, little time we are given, to be the best version of ourselves, to honor this life God has granted us, to honor God with sound speech, and to avail ourselves of the words that will promote good health and blessings for all those on whose ears and hearts they touch.

How might we truly answer the call to do good works when we use our words to judge others or ourselves? So often we describe ourselves in painfully cruel and critical language that only leads us to take on and live out those destructive characterizations. When we speak in such unfavorable ways to ourselves or to others, are we getting in the way of completing our good works – the purpose for which we are created? There is overwhelming evidence suggesting that we are. We are learning more and more that unseemly words depress our mood and deplete our confidence, and they also can destroy relationships. We need to find a way to attach to words that give life.

The course of history repeatedly shows us that people are more likely to lead fulfilling lives and achieve their purpose, when they are girded with words that are profitable, encouraging, promising, and offer hope.

To address my earlier question on how we may cultivate the habit of choosing words that bestow good health and impart life, I believe it begins with first setting an intention and a commitment, every day, to deliberately choose words that are pleasant, that bring about good health, and impart life.

According to several dictionaries, an intention refers to a state of mind that represents one's commitment to act in a certain way. What an honor it would be for each one of us, God's wonderfully made creation, to set an intention to use words that will nourish our soul and add to our life.

The Psalmist showed us, in Psalm 19:14, how we might begin this process, when he prayed that his words and his thoughts would be pleasing to God.

We too, could begin this process, by praying this prayer and making it our intention to target this goal as a daily practice.

Chapter 2

Speak to Live

"Death and life are in the power of the tongue: and they that love it shall eat the fruit thereof." Proverbs 18:21

Over a lifetime of teaching, coaching, counseling, and learning, I have come to realize that most of us, including me, consistently underestimate the power in our words, whether those words are spoken or unspoken. From time to time, I have heard some people say, "I will not put this [negative] word, or that thought in the atmosphere". Some of these very people go on to utter words of doubt, or statements of fear, and negative imaginings, then hold their breath and hope those words do not come true.

The Proverbs tell us that death and life are in the power of our tongue (Proverbs 18:21), or in the words that we speak, whether silently as thoughts to ourselves, or out loud, from our mouths. We indeed have power over death and life with the way that we speak and the words we speak.

If we took a moment to contemplate, I believe that we would agree that the words or thoughts we choose to think or speak, lead us to flourish or flounder. These words also reveal some deep-seated beliefs we hold about ourselves and the world around us, and as a result, they hold significant power over our lives, they dictate our actions, and they determine what our minds deem as possible.

Joy is a close friend and a woman whose words and insights have bolstered me over the years. She is one of the stars in my circle of friends, with her life-affirming, uplifting, words of optimism and hope. One evening, she told me of an event that would set the wheels of this book in motion. Joy had awakened that morning and prepared to ready herself for work, just as she had done every morning for the past 18 years since her first child was born.

Each morning, in anticipation of the day ahead, she would launch into her habit of first sitting for a few moments in silent meditation. Then she would begin preparing breakfast for her school-age children, so they might have a healthy meal to start their day.

Just as Joy was starting her morning, she felt the thunderous pounding of her heart and felt her chest tightening and her lungs choking for air. She recognized the onset of panic. *"There was tightness in my chest, and I could hardly breathe. I knew something was very wrong. I was puffing and sweating, my arm felt heavy and it occurred to me I could be having a heart attack."*

17

Joy said she thought that she might die as she took a seat on a chair at her kitchen table. It was early in the morning, she recalled. It was approaching the time of day when her youngest child would at any minute come running into the kitchen, so his mom could take him to school. Joy stated, *"I told myself, 'I will not die'. Not now. No way will my child find me dead at the kitchen table."* She recalls feeling her body getting weaker and it was becoming more and more difficult to draw a single breath. During that episode which might have felt like the beginning of the end of normal, Joy willed herself to envision her son heading off to college in future years.

She could have formed many thoughts to reinforce her fear. She could have given way to agonizing worry, or she could have allowed her mind to nibble away at any remaining vestiges of hope. Either of these actions would have led to increased anxiety and dread. Instead, Joy chose to think of the outcome for which she had secretly wished.

She thought of her young son, growing up, attending college, graduating, and pursuing his own dreams. It was a future she wanted to experience. She thought of herself being there to witness this part of her life, and she knew she needed to live. She did not want to die. Then she told me, *"I decided, this is not the way my story will end, this will not be my final narrative. I will not die. I will live."*

Joy continued sitting in the chair and rather than panic, she began to give her body the air it needed. She willed herself to slow her breathing down by taking deeper breaths. She asked God to save her life and allow her to live so she could see her youngest son complete college. She remained still and focused until she felt calm enough to move. Once she was able, she got herself ready and was able to take her son to his middle school. Joy travelled the five-minute drive to her son's school, and then she drove herself to the doctor's office. The doctors treated her and now more than 15 years later, the ingredients that give character to her existence and her interactions are filled with favorable speech that gives life and promotes health.

Joy's story is one example of how the quality of a person's life is influenced by the script or the narrative we create or repeat to ourselves. The Holy Bible tells us this is so. Neuroscience and the study of the way the brain functions, tell us that this is so. Psychology which sheds light on human behavior and the connection between the mind and the body, also confirms that this is so.

Research produces compelling evidence that people can, in fact, will themselves to live... or die. Medical doctors have reported witnessing persons who, with a positive prognosis, and while being prepared for surgery, have died, due to having constructed and held fast to a narrative that left them convinced they would die. This account by no means intends to suggest that people with a positive outlook do not get sick or die. However, we need not declare death over ourselves when Jesus gives us abundant life (John 10:10). The words we speak have life-giving or life-taking power. That morning, Joy's words and her fervent prayer, were a declaration of life.

On its website, the Mayo Clinic has posted that a person's narrative, or the stories they tell themselves, can yield health benefits if they are positive, or can lead to harmful results if they are negative.

When the grandmother of my friend Alex, was in her late 60s, she was diagnosed with a cancer that would certainly have scared many women. This diagnosis happened at a time when cancer for many was the equivalent of a death sentence and she was given a mere six months to live. This grandmother was also a matriarch in her family, full of life, and devout in her faith. She decided to live her life as though she had not been diagnosed. She kept her *joie de vivre* and chose to embrace and enjoy her life with the people she loved. She and her family reaped many benefits as this woman, mother, grandmother, and matriarch, fully *lived* each day until her last, which was years later than the doctors had predicted.

It is appointed unto each of us a time to die (Hebrews 9:27). Yet, with the power of the tongue, we create narratives about what is decidedly possible for us, and we do so in ways that can lead us to live spirited or lackluster lives and cause us to flourish or flounder.

Before deciding to write this book, I had not realized that my own narrative was tearing me down. "What if" was the lead-in to many of my own faulty thinking. "*What if this thing happened*" or "*What if that thing did not happen*" was part of my routine, and with each "what-if", I was sowing, at a subconscious level, seeds of doubt, distrust, uncertainty, and fear. When unchecked, these seeds were blooming into debilitating worry. I had told myself and others that I was preparing for the worst and I was being practical and forward-thinking. I have since come to learn that there is a vast difference between preparing and worrying.

One day, my girlfriend Vi, interrupted my "what-ifs" and asserted with an air of what sounded like irritation. *"You're such a pessimist passing yourself off as a realist! Gosh!"* In my mind, the "gosh" underscored her annoyance and my own thoughts came to a screeching halt. I was not a pessimist. I was definitely not that person, or so I thought.

Vi elaborated and I began to slowly recognize a hint of truth in her words. The fact is, I had been someone who spent a lot of time imagining the worst possible scenarios, and then I would pass hours devising a strategy for how to handle them. However, quite often, these imaginings would lead to a form of anxiety, worry, or worse. These moods would alter my mind and leave me vulnerable to depression. Vi had challenged me with her statement.

The power of death and life is in the words we speak, and I had been dishonoring my life with my pessimism. I decided in that moment, that I would need to change my language and my narrative to embrace life-giving words. "What if I changed my thinking and started to believe something positive was possible?" That idea began my journey to intentionally transform my speech and the words I use. This attitude has helped me to look for the best in people and situations. With this internal power that I have come to acknowledge, I now make up new stories. My narrative has gradually changed from, "What if I don't get that job", to "What if I get that job" to, "I will get that job". I am not perfect, yet I have made significant progress. To be clear, things do not always work out like I think they should; however, I no longer make myself sick by imagining the worst.

Our words have power to enhance our life. From the moment I set the intention to use words that promote good health and impart life, the conviction behind my words increased. A similar conviction for life infused the words that were spoken by Joy and by Alex's grandmother.

Chapter 3

Honor your Mind as you Honor your Body

"Finally, brethren, whatsoever things are true, whatsoever things are honest, whatsoever things are just, whatsoever things are pure, whatsoever things are lovely, whatsoever things are of good report, if there be any virtue, and if there be any praise, think on these things."
Philippians 4:8

Another seed that sowed the impetus for my commitment to change my words and my own narrative came in the form of a timely reminder from a friend. In one of our conversations, she gently stated, "You must remember, your body is the temple of the Holy Ghost" (1 Corinthians 6:19). *"A temple?"* I wondered. *"How do the words I utter affect the temple of the Holy Ghost?"*

For a number of different religious practices, a temple is the name given to their place of worship. Whether it is among Abrahamic religions, eastern religions, or among contemporary religions, a temple refers to a structure that is set aside for a sacred and serious purpose. It is a symbol of love, meant to shelter, protect, house, and comfort many persons. A temple is intended to provide opportunities for stillness, serenity, acts of devotion, and communion with God. It is meant to help prepare people to enter into a mindset of worship. Temples are often welcoming, and invite those who occupy, to quiet their minds, to focus their thoughts, to be still, and to meditate on the things God would have us know. As a result, many people take great care to ensure their temple and all it symbolizes, is kept in pristine condition to facilitate its purpose.

If the body is indeed a temple, it must be preserved, and its beauty must be maintained to advance its purpose. It must be able to function as a conduit for peace and comfort, and it ought to be an instrument for worship and communication with God.

The human body also houses the mind which generates thoughts. These thoughts may be healthy, or they may be destructive. As such, a wise person would aim to nourish the body with healthy, life-boosting, thoughts, and in so doing, we would be helping to preserve the beauty and the function of this temple that is our body. Unfortunately, we commonly dishonor our body when we dishonor our mind with thoughts that are destructive or thoughts that do not edify.

We have the ability and the power to choose our thoughts. When we feed our mind with unhealthy or unpleasant words and thoughts, we damage our body (which is the temple)'s capacity to heal and function as it was intended.

To feed the mind, we are directed to focus on specific, wholesome, subjects. God's Word challenges us to focus our minds on things that are true, honest, lovely, and of a good report (Philippians 4:8). The mind will flourish when it develops good life-giving thoughts and words. The mind when it is flourishing will help us achieve our goal of a life that produces good works, and so we must ask ourselves, what are we doing to keep our temple in the best possible state? How are we ensuring that we are maintaining ourselves, so we are poised to produce good works? How are we ensuring we remain in a position to do our best work and live the best version of our life?

Many of us are vigilant about ensuring our vehicles, technologies, equipment or other tools, are kept well so they may operate smoothly and function properly. Many of us also try to eat a balanced diet to nourish our bodies which help us function effectively. Similarly, we might aim to honor this temple – our body, by guarding the mind and feeding it, by meditating on pleasant, lovely, honest, healthy, life-giving thoughts.

The mind functions like the main operating system of the body. When it is in peak condition, the body is able to function efficiently and effectively. The body is also able to accomplish its goals and maintain its best possible state. When the mind is fed healthy words, and is reinforced with positive, life-giving thoughts, it develops into a secure, strong powerhouse. When a mind is deprived of healthy words, and instead, is allowed to feed on doubt, fear, disbelief, unforgiveness, judgments, and other elements that destroy, it deprives the body of its ability to function at its best. It robs the requisite energy and motivation that the body needs to move forward. Over time, the body, which is the temple, loses its ability to function as God intended and it loses its ability to produce good works.

We are also charged, in Ephesians 4:29, to protect our mouths from any corrupt communication, and rather, to only allow words that are edifying and instructive, so that they may minister grace to hearers. Hearers are everyone within the sound of our voice. Each one of us is a hearer of our words, whether or not they are edifying.

One goal of this chapter is for each of us to increase our willingness and motivation to the loving preservation and honoring of our temple, by guarding our mind from unhealthy habits. It is a guide to help us develop a deliberate practice, and lay a new foundation, habit by habit, word by word, until we make it a natural practice of nourishing our mind, and honoring our body, in order to live our best life and produce good works.

Chapter 4

Words have Power

"A good man out of the good treasure of his heart bringeth forth that which is good; and an evil man out of the evil treasure of his heart bringeth forth that which is evil: for of the abundance of the heart his mouth speaketh." Luke 6: 45

Words transform! It is the reason we use them to convey our passions, our emotions, our feelings, and ideas we wish to express.

From all that I've seen and experienced, I have come to accept and appreciate the authority and governing power of words, whether they are spoken out loud or whether they are kept hidden in our mind as thoughts. In fact, there is no greater model of the power of spoken word than in the account of the earth's creation as told in Genesis in the Holy Scriptures.

The blueprint for our world's existence is - God spoke, and the world came into existence. God said, "Let there be light;" then there was light. He said, "Let there be a firmament in the midst of the waters;" and the sky was created. God said, "Let the waters under the heaven be gathered together unto one place and let dry land appear;" and the earth separated from the seas. Trees, plants, herbs, and grass; land animals, birds, fish, the moon, the stars, the planets, and humans were created only after God commanded them so (Genesis 1 – 2).

Notice that the scriptures did not merely state that God created the earth and all the things in the earth, even though this is essentially what occurred. God is, after all, sovereign and commands things to exist. God existed before the beginning of the world and will exist beyond time as we understand it (Revelation 21:6). The scriptures could certainly have stated that the world was formed in six days. Instead, I believe God wants us to recognize that words have power to transform and make things happen, and that is why we learn that Jehovah, the sovereign Creator used words to speak and order things into being.

As we read through the Holy Scriptures, we also learn that John, an Apostle of Jesus the Christ, declared "In the beginning was the Word". John continued to say, "the Word was with God and the Word was God" (John 1:1), which suggests that all things started with a word ("let there be..."), and all things began with the Word. All of life as we know it, in fact, all of creation, everything we experience, all started with the Word, which is God, and it all began with a word that was spoken by God.

Throughout the Bible, miracles and healings are performed with a word. Parables, stories, affirmations, declarations, and blessings are conveyed with words. Lies, blame, judgments, complaints, and remorse are expressed with words. Truth, forgiveness, kindness, hope, and affection are communicated with words. Not only with words, but with actions too; and our actions when in synch with our words, make those words even more forceful with their impact.

We are mortals. We are not, nor will we ever become God, which means we cannot do all that God is able to do. However, just as God created us in His own image and His words have power, so I believe that we, in the likeness of God, would do well to acknowledge that our words have power.

Power is in the words that we choose to construct the language we use, regardless of the manner in which we communicate. Power is also in the words we form with our thoughts. We express our thoughts and ideas in the language we internalize, as the 18th century English writer and lexicographer, Dr. Samuel Johnson said, "Language is the dress of thought." Jesus told the crowds who had gathered to hear His teachings, that both good and evil people alike, when they speak, they reveal what is in their heart, when He stated, "...of the abundance of the heart his mouth speaketh" (Luke 6:45).

Healthy words can push us forward with motivation and encouragement; they can uplift us and bring joy to our hearts. Toxic thoughts can hold us back with fear, can dampen the spirit, and can drain the power that God has given to us.

Whenever I use words that cause hurt to me or others, then I know that all is not well on the inside. I have come to admit that when my words were harsh and critical, my heart was experiencing pain. Consequently, if my words were causing hurt to others, then I was unwittingly hurting my inner spirit and therefore defiling the temple of the Holy Spirit. When my words instead are kind, gentle, uplifting, and encouraging to myself or to others, they represent evidence of an abundance of a healthy heart, a whole mind, and a dwelling place fit for the Most High God.

I now use the scriptures as a guide and a roadmap of instructions by which to live my life. The Apostle Peter offers a guide in 1 Peter 3: 10, when he writes that those of us who love life and want to see good days must watch our words. By keeping these instructions close to our heart, we might increase our willingness and our motivation to improve the quality of our speech.

Instructions like these have turned me on to the power and the benefits of life-giving words to bless and to heal, the self and others. These instructions also help me understand how to become more consistent with my own practice of choosing to use life-giving and life-sustaining words. Inspired by the Psalmist, I am guided to make changes necessary so I may live the best version of my life.

To that end, one of my prayers continues to be "Let the words of my mouth, and the meditation of my heart, be acceptable in thy sight, O Lord, my strength, and my redeemer." (Psalm 19:14).

Chapter 5

Renew your Mind

"And be not conformed to this world: but be ye transformed by the renewing of your mind, that ye may prove what is that good, and acceptable, and perfect, will of God." Romans 12:2

In case you are wondering whether science supports the link between our words and a healthy life, it does. Remarkably, although not surprisingly, science affirms that our words have a significant and life-changing impact on our DNA and the health of our brain. There is a deluge of research that confirms we can, indeed train our brain. There is overwhelming evidence that the words and thoughts we repeat and rehearse, can cause our brain to develop or to decay. This concept bears a striking similarity to the power of life and death that exists in our language. This idea of the brain's ability to change, heal, and renew itself was first made known in the Word of God.

In Paul's letter to the Romans, (Romans 12:2) he encouraged us to change ourselves and live our best lives, by renewing our minds, so we could live the life aligned with God's perfect will for us. God's will for us, has always been for us to have a rich and ample life, (John 10: 10). All of this was declared, long before science opened to the notion that a renewal of our mind was even a possibility.

DNA

Humans and most living organism contain DNA, or deoxyribonucleic acid, which is a hereditary material found in the cells of our body. DNA communicates genetic instructions that tell the body how to develop, how to grow, how to renew itself, and how to carry out its other functions. It even communicates instructions for ceasing to grow or live. Science is helping us learn that we have the ability to influence some of the instructions that our DNA communicates.

Much of what we automatically say or do is guided by the thoughts we repeat to ourselves, like a mantra. These thoughts become the code that guides our own internal navigation system and our DNA eventually bears the imprint of that narrative.

There are people who are sick, weak, and inflamed in their bodies, who are this way due to ailing thoughts or words that they repeat over and over to themselves. Renowned neuroscientist and author, Dr. Carolyn Leaf[1] reports that our DNA changes shape based on the type of thoughts we practice. Dr. Leaf writes that negative thinking like bitterness, unforgiveness, or other thoughts that increase fear or other negative feelings can cause our DNA to change its genetic expression, which changes our brain's wiring in a negative direction. The brain translates these thoughts into stress and stress makes our body sick.

Science is also teaching us that this damage does not need to be permanent. The harm may be corrected when we begin to practice thinking that inspires hope, kindness, love, blessings, affection, and other positive feelings.

Besides DNA, another complex, conveyor of information in the human body lies in the workings of the brain. For over 2000 years, the great scientists have been interested in understanding the way the brain functions. For most of this time, it was generally accepted that the brain remained rigid for approximately the first one-third of a person's life, after which time, its functioning would only decline and degenerate until it could no longer serve us. However, one of the most significant breakthroughs in the world of science occurred when the scientific community, consisting mainly of neuroscientists, began gaining more understanding and greater acceptance of the flexibility of the brain's functioning.

According to the National Institutes of Health (NIH), the term "neuroplasticity," also referred to as "neuronal plasticity" had already been coined by the "father of neuroscience" Santiago Ramón y Cajal (1852-1934).[2] Cajal had begun to document changes in the structure of adult brains and offered that new brain cells could replace older, damaged cells, as opposed to the previously held belief that the adult brain cells were rigid, and once dead, they could not be replaced.

In the mid-1960s, with the help of brain imaging techniques and groundbreaking research, scientists and medical professionals began gaining broader access into the brain. The term "neuroplasticity" came to describe changes in adult brain cells and neurons, based on internal or external stimuli. In the late 1990s, reports emerged that even the stress that we experience can damage or kill neurons in the brain.

We now live in extraordinary times, where research findings are helping us learn that the brain has the remarkable ability to regenerate, to renew, to heal, and to learn, by forming new brain cells, developing new pathways, and forming new connections. These abilities of the brain give us, humans, the capacity to change our patterns of behavior and thinking, and to transform our lives into the best versions of our selves. This transformation can lead us toward an abundant life. Neuroplasticity and neurogenesis help clarify parts of the brain's functioning.[3]

Neuroplasticity

As alluded to in an earlier section, neuroplasticity is a word comprised of two concepts: neuro – which refers to the system of nerves; and plasticity – which refers to the ability of matter to be malleable and to change. Therefore, neuroplasticity refers to the ability of the brain to change and adapt by forming new connections.

We reinforce our brain's neuroplasticity, whenever we make the intention to practice a new habit or to try a new way of performing a task. With each new intention, we increase our ability to create neural pathways or connections in our brain. Isn't this exciting news? This means that with the scientific breakthrough of DNA and neuroplasticity, we are getting to understand that we indeed have an ability to retrain our brain and renew our minds (Romans 12:2). This is another instance of science confirming the scriptures.

The brain's neural connections become stronger the more we use them. The connections that are already formed in our brain become weaker the more infrequently or inconsistently we use them. This is a reason why we complete some tasks on auto-pilot and other tasks; we think we just can't do. It is wise to engage strategies that will help us strengthen connections that reinforce healthy patterns of behavior and try to disarm those connections that reinforce habits that hurt us or do not help us.

Maud is an accomplished woman, intelligent, and has a knack for preparing in advance for the future. When her father was diagnosed with early-stage Alzheimer's disease, Maud decided to investigate activities she could do to reduce any vulnerabilities she could have associated with the disease.

Maud told me she wanted to learn something new, since she had heard that learning is one effective way of activating new neurons. The issue Maud faced was she had barely any time to take on a task of learning a new language or learning to play a new instrument. Armed with a speck of knowledge about how the brain functions, I suggested that she try to do small tasks differently. *"Get in your bed from the other side"*, I suggested. *"Wear your watch on your other hand. Drive a different route to work."* These were some of the suggestions we brain-stormed together.

A week later, Maud reported that she had decided to try getting in her bed from the left side, where in the past she had always entered the bed from the right side. It seems like a fairly routine activity, after all, nothing was blocking her entrance to the bed, however, something in this seemingly routine task had changed and she was no longer functioning on autopilot. Maud said she stood at the side of the bed staring at it for minutes, as she tried to mentally figure out how to get herself in the bed. This is a task she had done mindlessly, at least once per day for most of her life, and by changing one part of this activity; her brain had slowed down in order to communicate the instructions for this task. For several minutes, Maud stared in puzzlement at her bed, trying to navigate what should have been a very simple task. This experience is one example confirming that changing one's behavior can be difficult. By changing the way she had previously entered her bed, her brain needed to make new neural connections.

The more Maud would repeat this new task, the stronger the neural connections would become, until this new task would become routine. This action represents one way of waking up and renewing our remarkable brain.

The more we repeat new patterns of doing things, including, speaking, or thinking, we are creating new neurons and we are rewiring our brain for peak functioning. Science refers to this ability of the cells and the nervous system in our brain, to regrow and replenish themselves as neurogenesis. This replenishment and renewal are necessary for a long and healthy life. The more we repeat the new patterns, the stronger these neural pathways become. The stronger these neural pathways, the easier it is for us to carry out new and healthy habits. Thus, when we repeat a new habit, consistently, over a period of time, our neural pathways are strengthened and the habits we are learning become easier to do. This is a rather technical way of saying, we can learn any new behavior with practice, practice, and more practice.

In the same way, when a person is trying out a new behavior, that has not been practiced regularly or consistently, those neural pathways related to the habit are weak, and the new behavior does not come as easily. This is the reason we find it so much easier to continue with older habits. It is the reason changing any learned behavior, as we get older is not as easy.

The analogy of hiking on a trail clarifies for me how we automatically choose familiar habits. Often when hiking, it is very easy to find the familiar path. It is well-worn and calls out to us, and we naturally and easily orient to that footpath. When we spot the hiking trail, not much forethought goes into our decision to mindlessly and automatically take the well-trodden path.

The hiking trail is like a familiar, automatic way of thinking or behaving. To change that thought pattern or that behavior, would require as much effort and deliberate intention as choosing to take an unused or different path. The well-worn path is more inviting because it is familiar, even if it is no longer serving us. So too are old habits, including old patterns of speaking, even if they no longer serve our purpose. Sometimes without thinking about what we are saying, we might be using words that cause harm, unconsciously.

Although this book focuses on the impact of our words; the regrowth of our brain's cells and the renewal of our minds, are helped when we consistently and intentionally practice other healthy behaviors.

Some other behaviors that help restore and replenish our brain health include:

Sleep:

The average adult can thrive well on 7 – 9 hours of restful, uninterrupted sleep per night.[4] Some people may require more or less. The idea is to practice the habit of sticking to a healthy sleep routine. [Sleep hygiene includes silencing noises, including sounds or light from television or other technology as we prepare to sleep.] The environment is changing fast and is overwhelming our brains as they try to adjust to present-day sounds. Our brains function efficiently in relaxing, nature sounds, like birds singing, crickets chirping, wind whistling, and rain pattering. The brain rests more serenely with those sounds, while the sounds of technology are more jarring. With each ping, alert, alarm, ring, or other type of notification, the brain responds as though an urgent alarm is sounding. For example, having your phone on alert when you are trying to sleep, keeps the brain jumpy and ready to act, whereas silencing those sounds increase the brain's ability to ease into a more relaxed state.

Movement:

One of my mantras I insist for my clients, states: *"movement is medicine"*. The World Health Organization, and every medical or mental health resource I have encountered, endorses daily forms of cardio exercises or other movement as having long term benefits on the body, the soul, and the mind. The Journal of American Medical Association recommends adults participate in 150 – 300 minutes of moderate activity each week. To begin, I encourage 20 - 22 minutes per day of aerobic movement (including walking, biking, running, dancing) to refresh and renew the brain's healthy functioning.

Life Habits:

Whatever we ingest, if it is bad for the body, it is bad for the brain. Things like excess sugar, excess caffeine, alcohol, or illegal drugs can hurt our brain's ability to restore itself. They can cause inflammation and impair the body's ability to flourish. This is especially true as we get older. Instead, I encourage reducing or eliminating sugar, caffeine intake, alcohol, and recreational drugs so we may gain better control of our mood, improve our brain's health and expand its ability to replenish healthy cells that it needs in order to help us thrive. Please be sure to seek the supervision of a licensed, medical doctor who will guide you to take medications in a way that will help you achieve your health goals.

Eating:

Healthy eating habits comprised of balanced portions will help us nourish our body and our brain. Eating should be done mindfully, slowly, paying attention to the look, taste, texture, and smell of the food. We need to eat attentively so that we may be aware when we have eaten enough. However, in addition to mindfully eating balanced, healthy portions, the National Institutes of Health, and the field of neuroscience encourage periodic fasting. Intentionally fasting from eating, can help our bodies heal and also gives our brain a chance to restore and renew itself.

By now, you may be seeing how the human body is interconnected. The mind, body, and spirit are inextricably joined together. This means that any behavior or habit you practice that impacts your mind, body, or spirit, will surely impact your mind, your body, and your spirit.

Chapter 6

Watch your Words

"A wholesome tongue is a tree of life: but perverseness therein is a breach in the spirit." Proverbs 15:4

In addition to food, and other substances, we also feed our brain with the types of words and thoughts we develop into narrative, as well as the quality of ideas and images we allow into our psyche. By being intentional and purposeful with the way we talk to ourselves and feed our minds with healthy, life-giving, restorative words, thoughts, and narratives, we place ourselves on the path to develop a wholesome tongue and increase our ability to generate words of life. According to the Webster's Dictionary, perverseness refers to the act of going against that which is right or good. In other words, if we know that healthy words provide healing and life, and we go against that by practicing corrupt, bitter, angry, or disagreeable language, the scriptures say we are creating a breach in our ability to live an abundant life.

As we continue to learn about some of the workings of the brain, whether we want to accept it or not, science and the scriptures show us that words and thoughts have the power to change our brains and leave a lasting impression.

Neuroscientists and authors Andrew Newberg, M.D. and Mark Robert Waldman[5] are considered by many to be the world's leading experts on spirituality and the brain. Their research corroborates the findings that words alter our brains. Their studies have shown that words have the power to influence the expression of genes that regulate our physical and emotional stress. Whereas positive words strengthen the executive functioning of the brain, which is responsible for thoughts and language, negative language interferes with genes that play a role in protecting us from stress. In other words, perverse language impairs our overall functioning.

Another neuroscientist and Nobel-prize winner, Dr, Roger Sperry[6] further explains that the left brain which is primarily responsible for language, speaking, writing, logical, and analytical thinking, develops words for our narrative, it is the right brain which is the seat of imagination and creativity, that transforms these words to pictures, images, emotions, and feelings. The combination of images and emotions guide the brain toward a vision of what is possible.[7] With enough repetition, the brain and unconscious mind will attempt to make these images real. With enough repetition, neural functioning begins to change, pathways become activated, new connections are made, and our perceptions and perspectives of what is possible, begin to change.

While many of us may have had experiences that bring this concept to life, here is a documented story of one man who broke the 4-minute mile:

On May 1954, England's Roger Bannister[8] decided he would attempt to run the mile in 4 minutes, a feat that had never before been accomplished by any human being. In fact, many at that time, had believed that no human could ever run a mile in 4 minutes because something bad, like death, would happen to them. Furthermore, Bannister's chance of achieving this milestone might have been even more bleak when you consider that he had finished 4th in the 1500-meter race at the Olympics two years earlier. Bannister was also a medical student whose priority was studying and doing rounds, so he had relatively little time to devote to training on the tracks. Nevertheless, Bannister took upon himself, this challenge to run one mile in under 4 minutes. On the day of the race, it is reported, the weather conditions for running were not favorable.

Bannister ran the race, broke the tape and collapsed in his victory, knowing he had accomplished the unthinkable. In an interview post-race, Bannister said, his legs felt as though they were "impelled by an unknown force." [8] Roger Bannister broke the 4-min mile by completing the race in 3 minutes 59.4 seconds.

From the time the Olympic Games had begun in 776 B.C. to that day in 1954, no one had run the mile in under 4 minutes. Since Bannister, more than 1,000 people have gone on to run the mile in under 4 minutes. This is more than likely due to more people willing to believe or accept that this speed is possible, and their brains having begun to create a new image of what is achievable.

When asked to what he attributed his great feat, Bannister stated, it was less about the capacity of his lungs, or his heart, or even his physical ability to run at high speeds. Bannister attributed this accomplishment to his stretching his own mind into believing this feat was possible, and that he could do it.

This is the story of how one man told himself he could accomplish something that had never been previously done. Stretching the mind, believing things are possible, speaking life to ourselves, speaking words of great faith, are what our minds crave. Some areas of science describe this trait as a growth mindset, where people believe they can accomplish goals with dedication and deliberate practice. Regardless of what we choose to call it, we have a choice in the words or thoughts we embrace.

From science and medicine, we continue to learn that stress wears down our body's natural healing powers by attacking the brain's ability to function. When we practice harsh criticisms, pessimistic outlooks, or words of doubt and fear, stress increases in our bodies and our brains. The brain transforms these words, into negative imagery, and before long, we believe these doubts are in fact a reality. Stress hormones are then released and unwittingly, we begin damaging brain cells. This damage occurs even if the narrative we tell ourselves is not true. For example, when you make a mistake then absently say, "I'm so stupid", the brain reacts as though it is real, stress gets produced and the brain takes the hit.

The exciting news is that the brain is able to contribute to the healing process by communicating its imagined hopes, silent wishes, dreams, and visions for the future. The brain makes these images real and the positive imagery triggers the release of brain chemicals, such as serotonin and endorphins, which are natural tranquilizers, and which explain the relaxed feeling that we experience when our words reflect a positive narrative. So, when the scriptures say we have death and life in the power of the tongue, it literally has been proven as true. We have the ability to destroy or build up our lives with the words we speak or think.

Chapter 7

Reframe your Thoughts

"For as he thinketh in his heart, so is he...." Proverbs 23: 7

Psychology, which is the scientific study of the relationship between the brain and one's behavior, sheds more light on how the story we tell about our lives, affects the outcome we experience and the way we experience those outcomes. The sooner we recognize that we are part authors of our own life story, is the sooner we can decide which attitude we will choose to experience this life. I believe that God wants the very best for us and from His Word; we learn that He will give us what we need to thrive. Jesus said we should not worry because it's our heavenly Father's intention to give us the kingdom (Luke 12:32). Jesus also said it is His wish for us to have abundant life (John 10:10), and the scriptures remind us over and over that our heavenly Father will not withhold any good thing from those who walk uprightly (Psalm84:11). When we focus frequently on thoughts like these, aren't we better positioning ourselves to thrive? I know this is so.

Our thoughts influence how we make sense of our experiences, which then influence our moods, our feelings, and our behaviors, or the actions we choose, and it is one of the basic concepts of behavioral psychology. Have you ever noticed how two persons can have the same experience and tell about it in very different ways?

Two persons could be looking at a glass of water and seeing it as either half empty or half full. The contents of the glass are at the half-way mark, yet our point of view comes from what we tell our self about what we are seeing. Was the glass full before some of its contents were emptied, or was the glass in the process of being filled? The way we think about that glass may affect how we feel. Some people notice their emotions change based on whether they view the glass half-empty or half-full. Researchers have used this example to assess a tendency toward pessimism or optimism. So it is, we interpret events and experiences based on the thoughts we develop from what we imagine or believe to be occurring. Those thoughts go on to influence our perceptions and help us make sense about the way we view the world.

There are people who are troubled in their spirit due to circumstances in their life that have led to anxious thoughts, worry thoughts, fears, unwarranted guilt, or secret shame. When these issues become unmanageable, it becomes difficult for us to function at our best. Thus, within a behavioral model of psychotherapy, when a client wants to change a behavior, the mental health professional will try to understand the individual's thought patterns in order to help that individual reframe the thoughts that are distressing her/his spirit.

Dr. Alfred Adler[9] was a psychologist who worked closely with Dr. Sigmund Freud – the father of psychiatry. One of Adler's contributions to the field of psychology asserted that our perception, or the way we interpret events in our life, dictates how we construct the story of our life and how we respond to experiences. According to Adler, *"reframing"* is the process of learning to change negative habits of thinking by viewing our experience from a different perspective, or from a different viewpoint. (Maybe view the glass of water as at the half-way level, or view it as being half-way full, if either perspective will improve your mindset.) When we succeed in substituting negative thinking patterns with more positive ways of thinking, we help improve our mood and enrich our spirit.

There are people who are able to reframe disappointment into a blessing, reframe their tragedy into a triumph, and reframe their test into a testimony. Not by changing the facts or by lying to themselves, but by finding a new way to view a situation.

One example of the relationship between how reframing thoughts can affect our functioning, was portrayed in a 1997 film called Life is Beautiful.[10] When a man and his young son became victims of the Holocaust, the father used his imagination to reframe each daily experience for him and his son. The father pretended with his son that they were participating in a game they needed to win, and this game comprised of tasks. By framing the experience as lighthearted, the movie shows how both characters were able to build resilience and mentally survive. So, an experience that could have been terrifying and crippling was instead more manageable.

Although this film claims to be loosely based on the story of a Holocaust survivor, it also highlights a poignant example of behavioral psychology that our thoughts affect our resilience or our vulnerabilities and our abilities to thrive or to succumb. If we each take a little time to investigate our own life, I think we will find examples of times we too have practiced reframing our perspective.

This example does not aim to minimize the atrocities and the horrors that occurred during any holocaust or the genocide of any people. This example also does not mean to suggest that the act of reframing will lead us to survive every situation. The practice of reframing our words and our thoughts can however, foster positive emotions, which will influence how well we cope with difficult situations.

By changing our ideas or thoughts, we can begin to change the emotions and eventually the behaviors and responses that unconsciously accompany those thoughts. With this approach, professionals can help individuals develop or re-write a new story, with new words, and a new frame, that is coherent and consistent with their hopes and dreams. The new story or the new narrative becomes an integral part of healing and recovery.

Thomas Edison is one of America's most well-known inventors. While he is known for a lot of inventions, he also had a lot of ideas that did not materialize or come to light. According to the Smithsonian magazine, when Edison was asked about the many failures he experienced, he had replied, "I have not failed 10,000 times, I've successfully found 10,000 ways that will not work".[11] Now that's a powerful reframe of an experience.

We are primed to focus on threats and disappointments around us that we frequently fail to notice opportunities and possibilities. We each possess a basic survival instinct which manifests in the way we are conditioned to look for dangers. However, when we only focus on the hardships, the threats, the disappointments, and the dangers, we sometimes miss noticing the blessing, the opportunities, the resources, and the open doors that could minimize or neutralize the threats and help us thrive.

The story of Thomas Edison provides a glimpse into how the act of reframing can impact the thoughts we repeat over and over to ourselves, which will impact our spirit, our resilience, and our behavior.

There are people who struggle and lose their ability to function at their best. There are people who, sometimes due to major negative events in their life, may develop thoughts that make it difficult for them to thrive. Psychologists and other mental health professionals try to help individuals learn and practice reframing their ways of thinking if these thoughts are barriers to progress.

Psychology offers that clients can learn to reframe their stories into narratives that are more consistent with hopes and dreams that can move them forward to a desirable life. In this area, the field of psychology is catching up with the scriptures that have always maintained, we are as we think. We are also learning it is possible to change our thoughts and seek healing for unhealthy thinking patterns, even if it requires the help of a health professional.

Chapter 8

Show me your Company

"He that walketh with wise men shall be wise:
but a companion of fools shall be destroyed."
 Proverbs 13:20

Sometimes a beautiful flower garden grows and thrives in spite of the presence of a few weeds. Sometimes we might plant seeds in dubious places and are surprised at the plants that grow. The words we speak over the life of others or ourselves are seeds that we are planting that will yield fruit of some sort. It is said that when you plant the seeds of an orange you may expect to reap oranges, not apples or tomatoes. In other words, the type of seeds we sow will determine the fruit we will reap. When we sow words of kindness, goodwill, and possibility over our life, or the life of our family and friends, we should expect a harvest of the same. When we speak words of unpleasantness, strife, or discord, we should not be surprised when afflictions spring up.

You may know some people who have a long-held practice of sowing seeds of unpleasant thoughts or speech both to themselves and to others. These seeds, when they take root, can and do bear fruit of unnecessary shame, fear, insecurity, worry, and despair. However, these are not the fruits that God intended us to bear, since these fruits will cause us great suffering. The fruits with which God intends to adorn us include love, joy, peace, patience, kindness, goodness, faithfulness, humility, and self-control (Galatians 5:22).

If we are not bearing the fruits that God wants us to have, we need to begin today, to search out, find, and weed out the unpleasant words or thoughts we are allowing in our spirit. As we are learning, the Holy Scriptures and more recently, scientific research is helping us realize that all of the words we speak, whether they are harmful or whether they are healthy, can etch themselves on our minds, until over time, those words begin to support or sabotage the very life we are trying to live.

Thus, the reason we are reminded to guard our minds. It is imperative to our life that we protect our mind fiercely, so that only the best ideas will enter and take their root. Is there any more compelling reason for us to pay close attention to the people who surround us and what they are speaking into our lives?

There is an old saying I learned as a child, "show me your company and I'll tell you who you are". This saying reminds me of the verse at the start of this chapter that those who keep themselves in the company of wise people shall themselves become wise and those who remain in the company of the foolish shall come to no good end. The people in whose company we choose to remain can shape our views, the way we speak, the words we use, the way we view the world, the things we deem acceptable, and the things we believe are possible. Fortunately, by knowing this, we each can choose to be wise.

I dare you to ask yourself, in whose company are you and who is in your company? What ideas and thoughts are they siphoning into your spirit? Are they propelling you forward or are they holding you back with the words they are speaking into your mind? Are their words souring your thoughts or are they sowing seeds that will bear good fruit? What are the words they are speaking into your life?

Most of us have friends, acquaintances, and family members who are at different stages of their own growth and maturity toward the best version of their life. It is likely that we will spend time learning from each other. However, if we spend all or most of our time with people whose words trouble our spirit or contaminate our thoughts, it will not bode well for us. In Romans 16:17, Paul urges us to watch out for people who cause divisions and put obstacles in our way that are contrary to the teachings we have learned.

We must stay away from people who will poison our health with unhealthy words. We must disconnect from people who sow seeds of unpleasantness into our life. We must keep our distance from people whose words will spoil the abundant life that God wants us to have. And, we must be willing to sow into others the same seeds that we wish for them to sow into our lives.

Today, I am very blessed to have a remarkable family who now consistently sows seeds into the life of each other. Words like, "you can do it" along with a smile and nod of encouragement, is a common response even to a partially baked idea that someone is trying to pitch.

This example is of a time one of my brothers sowed a seed into my life. He was still in high school and found out that I, his much older sister, was pursuing a Master's degree. "Oh," he said, "I thought you were in school for your doctorate." I tried to ignore what sounded like disappointment or deep yearning, while I tried to gently assure my brother, I had no intention of furthering my education. In fact, as soon as I was done with my classes, that would be the end of formal learning, forever.

"You should do it, Denise", he said. His statement sounded like a blend of a plea tucked in a wish. I did not recognize it then, but those words were a seed. As simply as that, my younger brother had sown a seed, an idea, a possibility, a hope, a declaration, maybe even a prophecy over me. Those words he unknowingly planted, once they took root, had quietly germinated into thoughts. A shift in my mindset had begun and over time, I started to think that a doctorate might actually be possible. Someone who knew me had envisioned a grand goal in my life and spurred me to consider that maybe I could actually do this. In 2008, I graduated with my doctorate from Teacher's College, Columbia University. I do not know when I first began to consider this dream of a doctorate for myself, but it was certainly not before my brother spoke those words. Like an invisible thread, my brother's words had planted seeds to a new narrative, and this narrative had led me, guided me, and pulled me unwittingly along a course, to a dream fulfilled.

Sometimes the people with whom we surround ourselves can give us a well-needed nod of approval or encouragement and we can uncover talents we may not realize we have. Talents that can help us live an ample life.

Lee is a gifted writer and she uses her talent to ghost-write some impressive pieces of work, because she prefers to remain in the background. Ghost-writers often go un-credited and unacknowledged, because they take content and transform it into a masterful piece of literature, only to have the client put his or her name as the author. Lee has also made a great effort to shy away from social media and was often scolded by well-meaning friends and colleagues for not having a public presence. "You have so many talents," they told her, "yet no one can find you!" When she reflects on her foray into social media, Lee recalls at first, she felt nervous, embarrassed, and like a misfit. Lee described it as being at a party where everyone knew she did not belong.

However, her "company" was the people in Lee's life who cared about her and wanted to see her succeed, so they continued to encourage her. Eventually, because of these seeds of encouragement, Lee began to build an online presence. Then one day, Lee got a call from a friend she knew cared for her wellbeing. "Lee, I love your posts", she said, "they are fresh and interesting. So, where did your photographer's eye come from all of a sudden? I didn't know you had one. What else you got in that head of yours?" Lee thought, "A *photographer's eye*," she had never heard or thought that before.

69

Another seed had just been planted. Lee said that after that comment, she beamed. Because of her friend's encouragement, Lee's confidence soared a few notches.

From that point on, Lee said she ceased being intimidated by the fancy photographs and perfect galleries displayed by social media *"influencers"*. From that moment, she decided to have fun and develop a presence, so people in search of a writer, could find her. From that moment, she started to embrace her newly discovered, *"photographer's eye"*.

This type of shift is what a genuine nudge by well-meaning friends in our company can accomplish.

There are also people we perceive as having expertise whose words we internalize. Sometimes, we unknowingly adopt people's stories for our life, and weave them into our own narrative, and if it does not lift us up, it might lead us to have a life that is unfulfilled. Know this; everyone does not get the right to speak into your life.

While my brother sowed a seed of possibility in my life, and while Lee's friends sowed seeds that led her to broadcast her talents, these sowers could just as easily have planted seeds of doubt, just as Lisa's professor did.

By the time I met my sister-friend Lisa; she had successfully completed a Master's degree and had earned a series of promotions that landed her in a corporate leadership role in a Global Fortune 50 company. Lisa wished to pursue her doctorate, yet this dream was overpowered by a narrative that was far stronger and quite limiting. Her narrative, which had become her truth, was that she was a terrible writer. A college professor had told Lisa that she could not write, and Lisa believed that this person's authority, as a Professor, meant that the words she spoke had to be true. As a result, Lisa convinced herself that she could not earn her doctorate because, "*I just cannot write.*" That seed from the Professor could have permanently crushed Lisa's dreams and cause her to unintentionally reinforce a stranger's indictment over her life.

Over time, Lisa formed a group of friends who she called her Village. This 'Village' is an intimate group of people who encourage and sow words of life into each other. They are friends who lift each other up with their words. Thankfully, Lisa's story did not end with the narrative, "I cannot write". Her Village reminded her of her successes and pointed out to her that she could most certainly succeed in a doctoral program, the way she had been succeeding all along in her career. Lisa started to spend more time with her Village, and she allowed her friends to deposit new seeds in her life. They would say, "Lisa, go ahead and apply to the program." "What if I don't get in?" she would ask. "What if you did?" they would reply. They encouraged, cheered, believed, and supported Lisa toward her dream and a new narrative.

Lisa went on to earn a doctorate from Teacher's College, Columbia University. She also published her first book entitled, *Don't Abdicate the Throne*, written for every aspiring leader or anyone who is responsible for shaping the life or career of a young leader.

God wants us to encourage each other with our words (1 Thessalonians 5:11), not tear down each other's dreams. Encouragement is like oxygen, a vital element that supports and sustains us as we aim to stay alive. When there is not enough oxygen, we are not able to function or thrive, and eventually we die. The same is true of encouraging words. Encouragement lifts a person's heart and nudges a person forward. Without encouragement a person might feel forgotten, incompetent, and unimportant. When we lift up ourselves or others with encouraging words, we sow seeds of validation, motivation, confidence, and endurance that gently and steadily prod us toward our calling.

Sometimes we need people in our lives to help us change our words so we may change our narrative. Sometimes we need people who can walk in faith with us and see possibilities that our own narratives might blur. Sometimes we need people who will make bold declarations over our life so we may learn to walk in confidence and use our talent. Sometimes we need people in our life who can remind us and help us repeat and practice the words of a new narrative, especially if we are not doing it enough. Sometimes we need people who will help us move forward and bear the fruit of an abundant life.

May I urge you today, to limit your exposure to persons whose words are killing your dreams and draining your life? Seek instead after people, who have a wellspring of pleasant words that will sweeten your soul and bring health to your bones.

Chapter 9

Use your Courage to Change

"Have not I commanded thee? Be strong and of good courage; be not afraid, neither be thou dismayed: for the Lord thy God is with thee withersoever thou goest." Joshua 1:9

Have you noticed that we sometimes have difficulty speaking words of life to ourselves or to each other? As I started down this path of changing my words, I wanted to shout it everywhere and tell everyone, *"Change your speech and choose words of life!"* Surely, everyone would want this golden nugget that could improve our frame of mind, body, and spirit. The passion I felt about my 'good news' was soaring, until someone asked me, "What if people do not want to change their narratives? Because everyone does not want to do that."

"Wait, whaaaat?" I thought to myself. Then, "wait, whaaaat?" I said out loud.

I had not seen that viewpoint coming and it was an important one that I had not ever considered. Why would someone... anyone, want to remain in their suffering, when a change of words or a new narrative, would trigger a positive change in their lives? It is true that people do not have to change anything about themselves or their behavior that they don't wish to change.

The ability to recognize your own power to change your story or write a new story will not come naturally for everyone, and it certainly is not an easy task. When we are in a great place, things are going well, and we feel strongly as though we are achieving our goals, it is much easier to embrace a positive narrative of wonderful possibilities. At that time, it is much easier to make positive changes in our life. On the other hand, if we look at our lives and we are not satisfied with what we see, a close examination of our internal self-narrative might reveal a script mired in doubt, hurt, or uncertainty, and thoughts that leave us feeling stuck and unable to move forward. When we are feeling bogged down by unhealthy thoughts and a despondent mindset, even if some part of us has the desire, we might not be able to find the motivation to change our negative self-talk. After all, if it were that easy, everyone would do it.

For some people, it takes courage to change our language and create a new story. It takes sometimes, a sheer force of will to make a decision to change the story of your life. Sometimes it takes a deliberate effort to convince ourself that negative noise should not direct the content of our narrative. Sometimes this effort can feel like an uphill climb on a very slippery slope. The road seems long and the effort impossible... with ever-present taunts whispering seductively in our minds, *"what if I fail?"*

When telling your story, you are actually designing the template of how you see yourself. From talking and listening to thousands of people, I have come to learn that if the story you own, causes you to remain negative, angry, fearful, or hopeless, you have the wrong story. If the story you own helps you to feel confident, hopeful, and compassionate, you are on your way forward.

While it is true that people cannot be forced to change anything about themselves or their behavior that they don't wish to change, I am reminded that when God made a covenant with the children of Israel, as recorded in Deuteronomy 30:19, He said, "... I have set before you life and death, blessing and cursing: therefore choose life that both you and your seed may live."

Given all you have learned thus far about the strong link that exists between our words and our health, I hope you choose well.

For those who do not want to make a change ... you are making a choice.

For those who wish to make a change... you also, are making a choice.

We develop a new story by believing that more is possible for us. The path to a new story is by no means easy. The process sometimes requires getting away from a history of voices – some belonging to others, and some that are our own, whose limiting messages have stuck like super glue in our mind. The process of recognizing these ingrained narratives and changing them will certainly require for us to take tiny, baby steps toward change.

Sometimes it takes courage to change and choose life. Sometimes we need to search and uncover what the choices are, in order to make necessary change. Sometimes we just may need to look for the courage within, to change the way we speak. When we find it, we get to use it. Sometimes, we may just need to ask our Heavenly Father to do a new thing in us. Sometimes we may need to tip-toe our way to a new narrative, and yet, I believe the journey will be well worth the effort. It is not always easy to change our speech to words of life. It is not always easy, and yet it is possible.

The story we tell ourselves is made up of words that we have heard at some point in our lives. We may have heard these words from our parents, our teachers, the government, strangers, friends, social media, or other sources. When we assign these sources authority, we might notice their words begin to shape our thoughts, our ideas, our dreams, our perceptions, our confidence, or our doubts.

These words seem to replay themselves like a recording, over and over until they etch themselves into a narrative of our lives. Some words have even travelled down through the generations and inserted themselves into the stories we have come to believe about ourselves. Some of these words are insidious and malignant and tell a story of lack, hopelessness, and impossibility. When we attach to these words, we weaponize them, and use them in a way that hurts ourselves, or those for whom we care. The cunning trick of the devil is that sometimes the words that hurt are said with such guile, we may not even recognize that injury is being done. When this happens, it creates in us, feelings of doubt, fear, shame, despair, or unforgiveness, all of which can keep us stuck, confused, and losing our way. This is an elaborate trick of the devil.

Elise is an accomplished young lady who shared with me how she came to learn she did not matter and was never good enough. Her narrative and the words she used reinforced that message until she eventually found the courage to change the words she spoke into her spirit.

Elise was 14 years old when her much older relative began to inappropriately touch and do intimate things to her that are more appropriately done between wives and their husbands. This abuse occurred often, at times within a few feet of others, yet it seemed that no one saw or heard anything. Elise felt disgust with herself, as well as fear and shame after each predatory assault. She also felt confused about what she could do to help herself. Elise could not find a voice to describe how damaged and ruined she felt, however inside, she thought that she was impure, tarnished, and very inadequate. The acts she experienced were unspeakable, so shame further choked her into silence; and she kept the abuse to herself. Elise told no one, not even her parents, of the hurt and pain that grew inside. Maybe if at 14, she had believed she could have gotten some help, possibly her healing would have begun at that time. Instead, Elise's hurt and pain rested in her body and mind. The mind creates thoughts and words. Elise's pain gave birth to more seeds of shame, doubt, disgust, and fear.

Without realizing the harm this would cause, Elise had inwardly begun to formulate a story about herself that she believed would make sense of the pain she was feeling. In her mind, she would replay each of these assaults, and then she would confirm to herself that she was damaged and ruined. The more she rehearsed that story, the bigger the shame she felt. The more her shame grew, the less worthy she felt. Whereas her story about herself used to be that she was smart, beautiful, funny, and friendly, it slowly and unconsciously transformed into a belief that she was unworthy, unlovable, inadequate, and damaged. These indictments replaced affirming thoughts and words of life. This young girl had unknowingly begun tattooing these damaging words into the recesses of her mind.

Elise eventually found ways to avoid the predatory relative and keep herself safe. However, she had turned her new narrative of unseemly words into a weapon against herself. Furthermore, the more others continued to treat this relative with respect and affection, the more it reinforced for Elise the narrative that she was ruined, and that she was somehow to blame for the unspeakable things that he had done to her.

Elise's spirit was broken, and her soul was being damaged silently, by "the thief who comes to steal, to kill, and to destroy" (John 10:10). In her brokenness, she started to attach to ideas that she did not matter to anyone. She also tried to hide what she thought were visible flaws from every person with whom she came in contact. So, Elise learned to smile beautifully and work hard to keep the exterior of the temple appearing pristine. The inside, however, was in need of repair. That wicked thief had attempted to destroy the life that her heavenly Father had so masterfully and fearfully created for Elise. For a long time, that brokenness made it difficult for Elise to speak words of life to herself. She felt stuck and thought that others were passing her by and moving along with their life. Thankfully, Elise started to realize that her thoughts and her negative narrative were hurting her and holding her back. Over time she found a way to change her story. With the influence of some in her circle, she sought out and entered into a relationship with God. Elise learned that her Heavenly Father cared for her, that He had never left her, even when she was walking through what felt like the valley of the shadow of death, and as He promised in Isaiah 61, He would restore her joy and heal her wounds.

Elise decided to take God at His word that He would do a new thing in her. In the Holy Scriptures, Elise began to study and learn about the promises that God had for her. She held onto those promises and began to feel an internal shift, as she started to learn that God had only the best intentions for her. Armed with this knowledge, she began moment by moment to change her words, and reframe her story using new words that give life. This change took remarkable courage, which Elise came to realize she had possessed all along.

Elise changed her story after she learned to see herself the way God sees her. She came to embrace who God says she is. She came to accept that God loves her with an everlasting love. She began to profess who God says she is and learned to push away the thoughts that her shame and doubt had previously asserted. She started to accept God's forgiveness for herself and become unstuck.

So many, like Elise have experienced events that plant seeds of doubt and uncertainty in our minds. It might have been the teacher who said you could not write, or the parent who said, you would not amount to much. It might have been the friend who betrayed you, or the relative who abused you. It might have been the person who said *'people like you'* would not thrive or do well. Regardless of the source, the outcome is the same, when what gets planted in you, are seeds that bloom feelings of shame, doubt, bitterness, or fear.

When these events happen, we tend to question the very gift that God has placed in us, and we tell ourselves we will never be worthy of any good thing. Some of us even tell ourselves that God could never love us, even when His Word tells us that He loves us with an everlasting love (Jeremiah 31:3). We give in to thoughts of inadequacy and negativity. We tell ourselves a narrative of lies that has been woven by that thief who preys on the vulnerable, like Elise, seeking whom he can break down, crush, destroy, and devour. Like Elise, you and I have the courage within us, to change the words to our story, if we rehearse God's promises and ask Him to help us see ourselves the way He sees us.

Chapter 10

Speak Words of Faith

"And all things, whatsoever ye shall ask in prayer, believing, ye shall receive."
Matthew 21:22

Have you ever heard a pastor exhort the congregation to speak words of faith? And if you have, do you know what that really means? I admit I was more than a little perplexed the first time I heard that statement and I wanted to learn more.

One person from whom I have had the privilege of learning and getting to understand what 'speaking faith' really means is my Pastor and teacher. Dr. Philip Bonaparte is a board-certified, medical doctor, who is licensed to practice internal medicine. He is also a Bishop who serves as the senior Pastor of the New Hope Church of God in New Jersey. He is as committed to teaching, developing, ministering to, and helping people who seek a close relationship with God, increase their faith in God and lead more powerful lives; as he is to the practice of helping people heal their lives with medical interventions.

One trait that I have observed consistently in Dr. Bonaparte is his emphasis and reliance on God's Word. It has become clear to me that whenever I ask him a question so I may increase my understanding or gain insight into the mystery of life, he would usually say, *"Well, let's see what the Bible has to say about that."* He admits that he uses the Bible as the blueprint for the way he lives, the choices he makes, and the actions he takes. From the Bible, and under the tutelage of his own childhood Pastor and mentor, he developed three core practices that have

86

shaped his life, even until today.

The practices are:

1) Fasting and conditioning his mind to hear from God.

2) Praying and talking with God.

3) Studying the Word of God.

Fasting is a practice of choosing to deny oneself from having food and drink. Earlier in this book, we referred to the habit of fasting as a necessary practice for helping the brain and in so doing, helping the body restore and renew itself. There are times when a person may be required to fast from some or all types of food or drinks for health-related reasons. Fasting is also done for religious reasons, either as part of a religious tradition, or to engage in meditation and stillness in search of a closer relationship and understanding of God's purpose for that person.

The scriptures make many references to the power of fasting accompanied with prayer, as in Esther 4:16, in Daniel 9 especially from verses 3 – 23, in Mark 9:28 – 29, and in Luke 2:37. From these and other biblical examples, we see that fasting is used by individuals to seek God's forgiveness, His comfort, His help, and His guidance. These practices have also developed Dr. Bonaparte's Christian maturity, his discipline, and his penchant for speaking faith.

In spite of this discipline, Dr. Bonaparte is quick to remind that he is a man who has imperfections. Even so, he continues to visualize and speak life into outcomes he desires for himself and others.

I interviewed Dr. Bonaparte some months after I heard him deliver a sermon on the power of words. Naturally, this sermon was deeply rooted in the scriptures. It came as no surprise that he used several verses from the Holy Bible, some of which are also referenced throughout this book, to emphasize the significance of speaking positive, uplifting words, which build up, encourage, support, and edify, rather than tear down, discourage, alienate, and destroy. His teachings brought home to me, the timeless relevance of this quintessential message that we have liberty to choose the words that will guide us on a pathway to better health and a better life overall, instead of choosing a course that will generate angst and distress with the words we speak.

For Bishop Bonaparte, creating the right narrative is one of the core elements of his faith. As a young boy, he had dreamed fervently of becoming a medical doctor, yet after his biological father died, and possibly due to a financial shortfall that was created in his family, he no longer saw a clear path to his goal. He sought out scholarships to help realize his dream to become a doctor and was told by the Minister of Health in his country, that he would never be approved for a scholarship. To some people, this decision from such a level of authority might have signaled the final shutting of a door and the abrupt end to a dream. However, young Philip was already imbued with a faith and a staunch belief that his Heavenly Father who loves each and every one of us (Jeremiah 31:3), actually wants the best for each one of us (Luke 12:32), including him. As such, he continued declaring with faith and depositing prophetic words into his spirit about becoming a doctor, long before his acceptance into medical school was even a consideration.

While he did not know how this aspiration to become a doctor would come to pass, young Philip decided to accept God's promises that are revealed in the Holy Scriptures. Using the three principles of his faith: fasting, praying, and studying God's Word, he asked God to provide him the opportunity to attend medical school and carve out a way for him to become a doctor. He combined those prayers with a firm belief that God would indeed grant him his request. To that end, Philip's words of faith reflected his hopes and the measure of his belief. While waiting on God to open the doors for medical school, and still in his teens, Philip Bonaparte founded his first Church. He still believed that He would one day become a doctor. In the meantime, he continued ministering to people's hearts by sharing about his relationship with God.

Ordinary minds might not have been able to imagine the possibility of his ambition, and ordinary people might have chided him that his dream was a mere fantasy. After all, in the eyes of many, the path to his career in medicine did not appear to exist. However, from his youth to this present time, his act of speaking faith has been modeled after God's example of calling things which are not as though they are (Romans 4:17). The future Dr. Philip Bonaparte believed God had answered his prayers, so he allowed his faith to infuse his words and spoke with bold assurance until the evidence of answered prayers was manifest.

While still a teen, he was admitted to medical school, and during the early years, he continued to pastor the Church he had founded. From that young age, he had begun to carry out the act of healing people using a combination of ministry and medicine. After nearly 30 years of providing his expertise in hospital and corporate settings, in 2015, Dr. Bonaparte established a health center that provides free care for persons who have inadequate health coverage or limited access to proper healthcare.

Due to his accomplishments and his many leadership responsibilities, Dr. Bonaparte is often in positions where he is easily observed, and his leadership scrutinized. Given his visibility in the public's eye, I wanted to understand how his faith holds up when he faces challenges. What do moments of vulnerability or disappointment look like in a man who exhorts speaking faith? Does his faith always hold up?

As a man who is also pastor, husband, father, doctor, leader, and so many other roles, he has certainly experienced mistakes, hurts, setbacks, betrayals, disappointments, and other obstacles, both privately as well as publicly. I wanted to know how his language reflects his faith during times of difficulty and disheartening challenges. Below, Dr. Bonaparte describes some of the issues he has encountered:

"Sometimes when God gives us a vision, it might be preparation for a later time. However, sometimes in eagerness, we might push ahead and not get the results we expected. The worst thing is when the result does not reflect your intention. Also, one of the hardest things is being disappointed by people who you trust or people in whom you have invested time or effort. When disappointment hits, it may take a while to overcome and not give in. It is easy to question God and ask, "where did I go wrong?" or "how did I not see that coming?" At the time, you may judge that as a failure or as a low point. In those moments, it can feel lonely and difficult.

Yet, it is with a smile that I tell myself, "This did not take God by surprise." Then I say, "God, this did not take You by surprise. Show me, what do I do next?""

Bishop Bonaparte parallels his approach with his faith, to the story of David in Ziklag. David and his private army had returned to his home in the city of Ziklag, after the Philistine army had refused to let David fight with them. They found their city had been burned to the ground, and all their wives and children abducted by those who had raided the city. At first, all the men with David were heartbroken and distraught. However, their anguish soon turned to anger, and first they blamed then threatened to stone and possibly kill David.

He was afraid, yet the Bible says, David encouraged himself in the Lord (1 Samuel 30:6). It was probably during this time that David produced some of his songs, psalms and much of the work that has come to inspire so many people. Some Bible scholars suggest, it was also during this time, that David might have used his harp to play while he sang some songs of praise, like Psalm 34:1 which in part says, *"I will bless the Lord at all times: his praise shall continually be in my mouth."* It is possible he could have encouraged himself by repeating to himself, the very popular 23rd Psalm, *"The Lord is my Shepherd; I shall not want....yea though I walk through the valley of the shadow of death, I will fear no evil: for Thou art with me; thy rod and thy staff they comfort me...".* He might even have encouraged himself by repeating the popular Psalms 121, *"I will lift up my eyes unto the hills, from whence cometh my help. My help cometh from the Lord who made heaven and earth..."*

David chose to encourage himself, reframe his thoughts, uplift his spirit, and change his focus from concentrating only on his circumstances of despair, to speaking in faith and making preparations for the better outcome he desired. He eventually took action and banded with some of the very men who had been angry with him, to go after the raiders and bring their families home. In the end, David and his men brought home all the families, as well as loot from the war they had won.

Bishop Bonaparte describes the act of encouraging oneself in the Lord as an outgrowth of a close relationship with God. It is the act of speaking positive, encouraging words and possibilities over oneself that are aligned with God's will for us. He continues:

> *"Giving in to failure is not an option and even if failure happens, I believe there is something that God wants me to learn. Hardships will come, and when you don't know what to do, that is when you allow God to do*

93

what He does best. I believe that man's most extreme point is God's most opportune time to show Himself as God. After all, if we can figure it all out by ourselves, then we would not need God.

However, the more stuck we are and the more we are not able to figure things out, it's the more we need God. This is the reason I need my day-to-day walk with God. I have seen different things and have been through many things, but others in the Bible like Moses, David, Joseph, even Jesus also went through difficulties. When the devil tried to tempt Jesus (Luke 4), Jesus spoke words from the scriptures to put the devil in his subordinated place.

Also, I truly believe that God works all things together for good. I love the Lord and because I love Him, I know He wants the best for me. I'm His son. That's where trust comes in. The element of trust is more than simply believing. Trust also requires action, that falling-back experience where you close your eyes and fall back, and you are caught and held, to prevent you from hitting the ground.

94

> *It's not just saying, "God I believe you",*
> *it's saying, "God I believe you have my back"*
> *and you will not allow me to hurt myself. That*
> *is the challenging part of faith."*

This is how this Bishop uses a language of faith.

As a disciple of Jesus Christ, Bishop Bonaparte consistently encourages all who will listen, to make positive declarations a daily habit. His knowledge that God wants the best for him comes from one of his favorite verses in the scriptures: *"For the Lord God is a sun and shield: the Lord will give grace and glory: no good thing will he withhold from them that walk uprightly"* (Psalm 84:11). He says that remembering this promise, has allowed him to increase his faith from the time he was a teen to his present-day, adult life. He emphasizes with great conviction, that "we ought to ask boldly and definitively for what we want from God, and we should expect the same". He further clarifies:

> *"If you expect blessings, say so. If you*
> *expect a promotion, say so. If you expect*
> *healing, say so. Whatever good thing you*
> *expect, declare it. Use your words to prophesy*
> *the future you hope for and expect for*
> *yourself."*

Bishop Bonaparte's attitude and language of faith are consistent with the instructions from Jesus in Matthew 21:22, which states that whatever we ask for in prayer, if we believe it, we will receive it. Inherent in the declarations he upholds, lies a key element of belief. In other words, when we make a declaration of faith, it is essential to ensure that we truly believe we will receive that which we are declaring. It is imperative to have a firm expectation that what we declare, we will receive, and therein is our faith. Otherwise we are merely uttering words. If it is a declaration of faith, the Bishop cautions, it must be infused with belief.

For Bishop Dr. Philip Bonaparte, for me, and for many persons who are reading these words, the habit of making declarations and conditioning the mind to practice repeating positive, life-bearing words, coupled with the act of belief, is about speaking faith. According to Hebrews 11:1, faith is described as the substance or the attribute of our hopes even in the absence of actual, tangible evidence. In speaking words of faith, whether as a youth who believed he would become a doctor, or as a person who continues to make positive declarations over his life, Bishop Bonaparte, continues to transform his attitude, his faith, his language, and his approach in order to live an abundant life.

When we speak words, we are required to speak with the authority that God has given us with His Holy Spirit speaking and operating in our life. When we speak, we are required to speak words of life which come from having faith. Remember that faith is not a feeling or a mood. Faith is not born out of the way we feel in the moment since feelings can change rapidly. Faith is not based on things we know or have seen. Faith is a choice that we decide to live and speak by. Speaking faith is not an easy thing to do. It is certainly not easy to speak with confidence about things that we cannot see or feel. When he was a child, it could not have been easy for young Philip Bonaparte to speak words of faith, and yet he did it.

Do you ever tell yourself that you are reluctant to declare things which are not and speak faith, lest you get disappointed? If you do, you are quite normal. It often takes great courage to speak words of faith, yet, even when it is not easy, it is positively possible. Speaking faith is a way for us to speak life into ourselves. It is also a way we make the choice toward living the type of abundant life that God intended for us.

Section II

Now that you are learning about the impact of words, I believe you are motivated, and you may be ready to consider making a change. You may continue doing what is working well, and you may also choose to start some new habits.

This next section offers some keys for renewing and refreshing your wellspring of words, even as you continue on this journey of change.

Chapter 11

Keys for Keeping your Wellspring Refreshed

"Behold, I will do a new thing; now it shall spring forth; shall ye not know it? I will even make a way in the wilderness, and rivers in the desert." Isaiah 43:19

Changing how we talk to ourselves or to others is a journey that requires willingness and ongoing determination. This journey will not be a 30, 60, or even a 90-day endeavor; rather, change requires constant effort. Just take a look at how long we have been practicing negative self-talk and using harmful words against ourselves or others. Now use that as an indication of the time it might take to depart from those habits that no longer serve us, and turn instead, to new, more desirable patterns of behavior.

It is said that a boy came every day to a river behind his house and would observe a steady trickle of water hitting a rock, drop after drop. At first the drops of water did not appear to affect the rock. For many months, he would come to the river to watch the dripping water. One day, the boy noticed that the very spot where the water had been dripping, had become smooth, compared to the rest of the rock's rough surface. The boy was amazed that the steady dripping of water had made such a change to the surface of this rough rock. So it is, our steady efforts, when consistent, regardless of how small, can come to have a noticeable impact.

Change does not always occur due to a sudden or dramatic catalyst. In fact, change is often the result of a very gradual series of events. Every single drop of that water was necessary to smooth the rock, and yet, who can tell the precise moment when that spot in the rock went from rough to smooth? Who can actually point to that exact moment, when we finally let go of old behaviors and when our new behaviors become our norm?

The transformation from a negative, pessimistic, hurtful cadre of thoughts; to a more positive, optimistic wellspring of words that heal and uplift; is also a gradual process. It has long been said that practice makes perfect; yet, a client once told me that it was the promise of progress and not perfection that encouraged her forward. I believe that any practice will contribute to our progress, whether or not we achieve perfection.

Based on research from people's lived experiences, as well as scientific, psychological, and biblical studies, I have extracted some key ingredients that are themes that appear necessary to seal this journey of change:

I.   Willingness

For many people, that moment we realize that we need to make a change can feel uncomfortable and sometimes daunting. So daunting, in fact, that some even decide the discomfort is not even worth the effort of trying. Like a familiar hiking trail, the familiar patterns of behavior are far more comfortable than trying to do something new. This is so, even when we know that change would bring us great benefit, it can feel more comfortable to stick with the familiar.

Willingness describes an attitude of accepting the need to do something and being ready to take some sort of action toward doing what is required. Some people might only need to take small steps, while for others it may require many giant leaps. In either case, a willing spirit will move you closer to your goals than a mindset that is unwilling to try anything. When you are not willing to do so much as try even one thing, you will certainly miss opportunities to achieve many things. On the other hand, when you are willing to try and make a change you will increase your progress toward achieving your goal.

Most of us struggle with making changes. In the Psalms, we learn that King David often asked God to give him a willing spirit (Psalm 51). Willingness is a precursor to many successful changes and like David; you too may consider asking God to help you develop a spirit of willingness.

In my professional work, I help individuals and organizations prepare themselves to undergo significant change events. From individuals to groups, if they are not willing, no one can force them to make the mental shift needed for this change. The clients, to whom I provide psychological services, all make progress at their own pace, yet only when they possess at least some measure of willingness.

If you do not think you are willing to make a well-needed change, can you think of some things that might be getting in your way? List them here:

_____

_____

_____

The shift to willingness requires a shift of mindset and I refer to this as an attitude of "yes". This means we may need to stop telling ourselves what we cannot do and start asking ourselves how we will do what is needed. When we say "yes" to ourselves, "yes" to opportunities, or when we say "yes" to doing something that is helpful for us, we are opening our minds to possibilities. We are opening ourselves to receiving an abundant life. It is when you are willing to try... just try and turn your mindset toward making a change, it is then that you are able to identify what is that one thing you can do, or one step you may take to begin the journey of your change. After all, if we want to change something, we must change something and if we change nothing, then we should not be surprised if nothing changes. Consider that as you prepare for your change.

105

One thing that you can do is to say "yes" to yourself. Say yes to trying. Say yes to changing your words. Then make one more change. Having an attitude of willingness can ease you into becoming a better version of yourself.

What is one thing you can try to do, as you now say yes and are willing to make one change?

_____

_____

If nothing jumps to mind, would you be willing to start noticing how many times in a day your words bring hope compared to how many times your words bring hurt?

_____

_____

1 Corinthians 9:24 – *"Know ye not that they which run in a race run all, but one receiveth the prize? So run that ye may obtain."*

II. Acceptance

Many people are often prone to accepting what others say of them, without thinking, evaluating critically, checking the facts, or asking for clarity. This seems to be particularly true when the statements are negative and hurtful. Notice how much easier it is for some of us to push away compliments rather than criticisms. Some people also have a tendency to accept a negative, internal narrative they form, after something unpleasant, embarrassing, or even traumatic has happened in their life. Whenever individuals buy into a narrative that they are not good enough, are somehow defective, or ruined, or something bad might happen if people found out their flaw or 'glitch'; it seems that they have difficulty breaking away from that pattern of thinking. Ultimately, sometimes unknowingly, it can become the reason for remaining stuck in their lives.

Acceptance is another essential step in any change process. People with unhealthy habits e.g., substance misuse, overeating, gambling, overspending, or other unhealthy behaviors; must first accept that their behaviors are no longer helping them in their lives, in order to commit to the change journey. Psychology describes acceptance as a person's acknowledgement of the reality of an event, a situation, or a condition, as it is or as it happened. Acceptance does not mean condoning, being in agreement with, appreciating, or even liking the situation or condition. By accepting a situation, it also does not mean that apathy replaces your passion for something better.

Acceptance means acknowledging that moments are only moments and they do not have to last forever. This is especially important if we are replaying moments in our thoughts, and it is causing great sorrow. This is yet another example of why it is essential to examine and when necessary, reframe unhelpful thoughts. When we take the time to notice, we will see that moments do in fact change. In our willingness to accept our situations, we speed up our ability to recognize the way forward and the changes we can make. By accepting that parts of our language and the words that we speak have an impact in our lives and the lives of others, we can better increase our awareness of how to move forward to make the changes that are necessary.

Years ago, I was struggling with accepting that my life was not unfolding like I had thought it would. I was going through a difficult challenge the likes of which were bigger than I was able to grasp at that time. I kept saying, "I cannot believe this is happening. This makes no sense." It was as though I wanted God or someone else, to show me the missing piece of this puzzling situation, so that I could understand and therefore accept what was happening in my life. In the meantime, I was quietly criticizing and blaming myself and causing great harm to my mind.

One day, a dear friend firmly and caringly said to me, "*Sweetie, this is not acceptance. Repeating you can't believe it, is not accepting. It happened! It's horrible! It hurt! It should not have happened! You don't deserve it! Now let's see how you can move on.*" She continued, "*I know that God loves you. I love you. You are going to get through this.*" She was right and I did get through it. Notice how my friend's encouragement was filled with words of life that she poured into me. She also helped me to spot my words of non-acceptance. "I can't believe" or "I don't believe" or other words of disbelief about an event that has already occurred, is a sure sign of not accepting. By not accepting, I did not even find the willingness or have the mindset to change how I spoke about my situation.

In this life, there are some things we will never understand. If we are waiting to understand before we can accept events, then necessary change may never happen in our life. People who have had inexplicable, unspeakable things happen to them, may never get to understand why those things happened, and yet will need to acknowledge and accept that those things did occur, in order to move on.

What is your unspeakable? What are you having difficulty accepting that is keeping you stuck? Are you trying to understand something that makes no sense in the rational, logical realm? Would you be willing to try accepting that the unimaginable happened? Would you be willing to call it what it was - despicable, unfair, or whatever word that best describes your reality; and then, would you be willing to consider accepting that you deserve to get out of your rut, make a change, and get to something better? As much as possible, we need to accept the reality of our situations, regardless of how difficult or unpleasant those situations may appear. When we are willing to accept, we are ready to pivot, and we poise ourselves for progress. Acceptance also positions us to welcome and embrace who God says we are.

What is one situation you have had difficulty accepting?

_____

_____

_____

What are some words you use, that may be a roadblock to your accepting? (Mine were, "I can't believe...")

_____

_____

_____

Based on what you have already read, are there new words you can choose to use, so you may begin to change your narrative to words of life; and so you can encourage yourself toward progress in your change?

_____

_____

_____

2 Corinthians 4:8-9 – *"We are troubled on every side, yet not distressed; we are perplexed, but not in despair; Persecuted, but not forsaken; cast down but not destroyed"*

Asking for help

Asking is a way of making a request in order to gain something we hope for, desire, or need. Yet there are many individuals who are reluctant to ask for what they need or want, and they end up dealing with the consequences. Asking for help is often difficult when it causes a person to feel vulnerable, thinking that others might know of their lack. We might choose to not ask if we think that others cannot or will not give us what we want. We might also refrain from asking if we believe we have no right to ask. Yet, we are less likely to get the help or support we need or wish for if we never make our requests known. Whatever the reason, the scriptures point out that we have not because we ask not (James 4:2).

Previously, we pointed out the benefits of having people in your circle who encourage you with their words. The journey of change is difficult enough on its own so, having someone who willingly supports your goal of becoming better, makes a world of difference. Asking for support is a natural component of this change journey and can lessen some of the frustrations of this process.

Asking is a key ingredient in the change journey, whether you choose to ask for support from an accountability partner, a licensed professional who can provide psychological services, or your heavenly Father. Asking for help from God is akin to praying to your Father in heaven. We might not always get our requests granted, nevertheless, making the request is a healthy practice and a path toward progress.

If you have decided to make some important changes in your narrative, who do you want to ask for help?

_____

_____

_____

What specifically is the help you need to receive in order to move forward?

_____

_____

_____

Matthew 7:7 – *"Ask, and it shall be given you..."*

III.   Listening

Listening is an essential key that can benefit every area of our life. It certainly is one of the keys to any transformation we wish to make. Listening is also a choice that goes well beyond hearing. Listening requires that we remain still and attentive, so we may hear and understand all that is being communicated. At times we may hear sounds and choose to listen for their meaning or their value. We might also choose to listen and connect deeply with the message that is being conveyed. The world today has become loud and noisy with so many distractions that it is often difficult to hear or discern the meaning of important messages.   Disturbances from technology, traffic, people, and our own internal noises, can distract us, distort what we are trying to hear, and lead us away from our focus. Today more than ever, we need to search out and take moments to be still, so we may hear clearly.

Our bodies, including our heart and our mind also send us messages to which we ought to listen. When our body tells us it is tired, or hurting, or needs food, or rest, we benefit when we choose to listen and give it what it needs. When our emotions tell us we are feeling sad, or hurt, or disappointed, and we ignore them, we might be placing ourselves, repeatedly, in the same toxic circumstances. When we expose ourselves to words and language that uplift and fuel us, our bodies and mind respond positively, and we ought to crave more.

Similarly, I would urge you to tell yourself today, that you will no longer welcome in your spirit, any unpleasant words from yourself or others that drag down your emotions or veer you away from your goals and your purpose. For this journey of change, I encourage you to listen keenly to how words are affecting you and then decide what stance you need to take.

Whenever you ask someone for something, you ought to listen carefully for a response. If for your change journey, you asked for support or help from someone you trust, whether a friend, a mental health professional, or your heavenly Father, you might have a clearer sense of direction, if you were to remain still and listen for a response. It is the only way to hear so you may understand.

When I decided it was time to change from a negative narrative to a more favorable speech, I asked God to increase my awareness and my willingness to make the changes necessary. I started listening carefully to the words I was choosing, and I listened also to words other people were choosing to use around me. I held fast to words that encouraged and empowered me and began parting ways with language that did the opposite.

When we decide to change the language we use, we become increasingly adept at listening and hearing what words and ideas are being deposited into our spirit. We will also begin to notice how they make us feel. Listen and notice which words lift you up and hold on to those words. Rehearse them, study them, and make them yours. For words that pull you down, you may start to tell yourself, they are not your words, and they don't tell your story. The more you practice that type of in-depth, intentional, listening, in stillness, the easier it will be to formulate and practice new habits for your change.

As you aim to live your abundant life, as you choose to change the caliber of words on which you feed, take hold of moments to be still. Be still and listen keenly. Listen for new words and thoughts that will nourish you.

What is one thing you can do to increase moments of stillness in each day, so you may listen more for what you need to hear?

_____

_____

_____

Psalm 46:10 – "Be still, and know that I am God..."

IV.   Cloak yourself in kindness and compassion.

Kindness and compassion often go hand in hand for anyone on a journey of change, since the journey itself can be agonizing at times. Contrary to recent beliefs, showing kindness and compassion is not a sign of weakness; instead, they require formidable strength and inner courage.   The scriptures heed us to be kind and tenderhearted to each other (Ephesians 4:32) and they remind us over and over that to love someone, requires us to be kind and compassionate toward that person (1 Corinthians 13).   The scriptures remind us that God has given us power and He wants us to act with courage, not fear (2 Timothy 1:7). This tells me that we are masterfully designed and already equipped with the ability to show

116

kindness and compassion to each other and to ourselves. We learned earlier in this book that kindness and compassion increase cognitive flexibility in our brains, improve our mind's ability to function well, and boost our body's resilience.

As we continue on this journey of change, our speech must be sprinkled with kindness and compassion, even when it seems difficult to do so. Kindness helps to bring peace and harmony. The human body tries to be in equilibrium with itself since that is the best way for it to thrive, heal, and prosper. Constant fussing, unkindness, or cruelty creates disharmony and angst in our bodies and heart. It is imperative that kindness and compassion saturate our words and our thoughts, whether they are directed at others or whether they are directed at us. When we make it our goal to be kind and compassionate in all things, our language will change and the wellspring which is our energy source will be refreshed.

There is a friend from my childhood, who whenever he heard someone being harsh with themselves, would often ask, "are you being gentle with yourself?" When we are gentle with ourselves, we can show kindness to ourselves. It is necessary to be kind to ourselves, since that is the way to enhance our language. Take heed, however, that kindness or compassion does not mean steering away from doing the right thing. If you need to part ways with someone who is toxic in your life, it is possible to set appropriate limits with firmness, while being kind.

This idea brings me to a habit of speaking the truth with kindness. Have you heard someone say the most hurtful thing to another and then excuse it by saying, "I was only telling the truth"? When it is pointed out that their words hurt, they try to justify their actions by saying, "Well, the truth hurts". It is a healthy and positive practice to aim to speak truth, and it is even better to find a way to speak truth with kindness. For those who are willing to try, this change might be the start of a kindness contagion.

Who in your life, would you be willing to try speaking with words and a tone of kindness and compassion? I hope you will include yourself.

_____

_____

Think about a time when you or someone might have made a mistake. Was your instinct to respond with words of indignation? Try pausing and noticing the words you are about to use, then ask yourself, "are my words showing kindness right now?" Think of the last time you said something harshly to yourself... or to someone else.

Reimagine the scenario and write down how you might restate those words with kindness.

_____

_____

Colossians 3:12 *"Put on then, as God's chosen ones, holy and beloved, compassionate hearts, kindness, humility, meekness, and patience"* *ESV (English Standard Version)*

V.   Accepting Forgiveness

Much has been written about forgiving others. We have been told to forgive others as we would like God to forgive us, forgive 70 times 7 times, forgive and forget, forgive and never forget, and forgive and set appropriate boundaries. These are only a portion of some messages that have been drilled into our collective psyche, yet daily, we encounter people who have difficulty with forgiveness.

Forgiveness is a central theme of many religious practices. Forgiveness is also a central theme of psychological approaches. Leading health organizations around the world have conducted research that consistently shows strong links between forgiveness and an individual's physical, emotional, and spiritual well-being. Research also shows us that unforgiveness can perpetuate a host of unpleasant ailments related to one's physical, emotional, and spiritual health.

Original works like the Holy Scriptures, Simon Wiesenthal's *The Sunflower*, the *Book of Forgiving* by Bishop Desmond Tutu and his daughter Minister (now Bishop) Mpho Tutu, and *Forgiveness from the Heart* - a collaborative research by theologians, Dr. Wayne Solomon and Dr. Philip Bonaparte, are some titles that have provided readers with comprehensive guides to the understanding and practice of forgiveness.

Ironically, while the topic of practicing forgiveness has been discussed, researched, and encouraged extensively, very little has been researched, recorded, or discussed about people's difficulty with accepting forgiveness from others.

Why is it so difficult for us to accept forgiveness when it is offered? Or why is it difficult for us to doubt that we are deserving of forgiveness?

The scriptures tell us that God is good, He is ready to forgive, and He is plenteous in mercy to everyone who calls upon Him (Psalms 86:5). This means that the Lord is willing to forgive us, and there is no end to His mercy. God also promises that if we are in a covenant relationship with Him, not only will he forgive our wrongs, but He will also choose to not remember them anymore (Psalm 103: 8-12,

Isaiah 43:25, Jeremiah 31:34, Hebrews 8:12). These promises are evidence that forgiveness from God is the penultimate gift.

So why are we reluctant to accept God's forgiveness? Or to make it more personal, why are some of us reluctant at times to accept forgiveness from others?

Consider a person who says or does something egregious enough to offend or hurt someone. Eventually, the offender recognizes and even apologizes for the wrongdoing. The offender may make repairs, show contrition, and ask for forgiveness. The offended party says, "I forgive you," yet the individual who committed the hurt, seems unable to accept this pardon.

When a person cannot accept forgiveness from another, it can lead such a person down a slippery path of self-flagellation, self-judgment, self-punishment, guilt, blame, or shame, which can eventually lead to self-hatred and depression. When that person does not accept the forgiveness of a fellow human, one underlying belief may be that, she or he is not deserving of forgiveness. This type of language is pernicious and oppresses the human spirit.

The scriptures explain that the enemy who is also called the accuser of God's people (Revelation 12:10) weighs down on the human spirit and tells us we are undeserving of forgiveness, we are not worthy of pardon, and our misdeed was so bad that nothing can make it right. This is one way he destroys us and tries to interfere with our relationship with a God who loves us and wants the best life for us. When we choose to embrace guilt and shame over forgiveness, we in essence are allowing the enemy to put a wedge between us and God's care.

When was there a time you had difficulty accepting forgiveness from another person, even after that person had forgiven you? Try to recall your reasons for not accepting forgiveness. What were you telling yourself?

_____

_____

_____

When God's Word tells us that He has forgiven us, and we believe in our minds that we neither deserve nor are worthy of that forgiveness, what are we actually asserting? Are we affirming the lies of the enemy? Are we denying God's sovereignty? Are we refuting God's supreme authority to obliterate our wrongs and grant us forgiveness? Are we rejecting God's mercy? When we do not accept God's forgiveness, are we suggesting we know more than God who has already declared us worthy of forgiveness? These ideas are worth questioning so we may pin down what our thoughts are actually saying.

Keep in mind, the enemy uses shame, blame, and unjustified guilt as weapons to make us think badly about ourselves, and ultimately sink in despair. Let me clarify, there is guilt that is justified when we need to change the way we treat other people or when we need to change the way that we live. In that case, when we own up to our actions, make the repairs, and accept the natural consequences, we must let it go so we may move forward.

Unjustified guilt comes from faulty beliefs and assumptions that some people hold inside. It is usually an outgrowth of a critical or judgmental self-talk. Unjustified guilt describes feelings akin to guilt; however, when we explore the facts, we find no actual causes or valid reasons for those feelings. The Word of God instructs us to put our worries on God, and not hold onto them, because God does care for us (1 Peter 5:7).

It is both the giving and the accepting of forgiveness that helps to lift our spirits, strengthen our minds, and build our resilience so we may live. Giving and accepting forgiveness helps our whole body to detoxify from stressful, lethal thoughts. These acts help us become healthier, live longer, and function better. My assumption is that most of us, at one time or another, struggle with accepting forgiveness.

Let me challenge you with this reflection:

What would you do differently if you were to always accept forgiveness when offered?

_____

_____

_____

Remember that God's Word tells us that if we ask Him to, He will forgive us. How would your words, your thoughts, your emotions change, if it was embedded in your mind that you were forgiven?

_____

_____

_____

What reminders can you say to yourself that will help you consistently embrace and accept forgiveness?

_____

_____

_____

Psalm 103:12 - "As far as the east is from the west, so far hath he removed our transgressions from us"

124

VI.   Focus your Vision

It is said that highly skilled race car drivers take the curves at high speeds by visualizing their course and by training their focus on the speedway before them, rather than the wall that flanks the perimeter of the track. When race car drivers, driving at speeds of over 200 mph, focus on the wall that is at the periphery of the speedway, they are more likely to crash into it. On the other hand, when they are aware of the wall and keep their focus on the track that is before them, they are many times more likely to remain on course. What then, does auto racing have to do with changing our language?

If those walls are a metaphor for the things we need to avoid, what are the walls in your life? What are the threats, the dangers, the worries, or the fears you think exist, and with which you want to avoid a collision? Are you so fixated on their presence; that you forget to focus on the course that is right before you which will lead you to the outcome you desire?

Highly skilled male and female athletes are one group who understand and incorporate the power of a positive narrative. They visualize and then create the narrative for the outcome they desire. We, the spectators get to witness the realization of what they envisioned. One athlete, who was famous for this behavior, was boxer and former world heavy-weight champion, Muhammad Ali. According to Ali, he referred to himself as "The Greatest" even before people ever knew who he was.[12]

One highlight of Ali's talents, rested in the way he would visualize his victory in the ring, and would have often predicted the round in which he would beat his opponent. By the end of his career, Muhammad Ali is said to have won 56 of his 61 fights.[13] By the time of his death, the world had come to refer to Ali as "The Greatest".

Instead of projecting our hopes and dreams, quite often, our words reflect the threats and dangers that we perceive around us. We might tell ourselves:

"I can't take that chance; I will get hurt"

"I can't try out for that job; I will get shot down"

"I can't try, I will fail"

"I can't put myself out there; there are others who are much better than I!"

… and so on, and so on.

We are learning more and more that if this is the type of content that represents the nature of your speech and the narrative you embrace, then the things you say, will come to pass and:

You **will** get hurt;

You **will** get shot down;

You **will** fail;

You **will** miss 100% of the chances you never take; and

You **will** only perceive others as better than you.

The language we use often has a prophetic vein, and we tend to manifest outcomes we envision in the way we speak.

On this journey of change, who do you envision you are? What are the desires you dream for yourself? What is the life you wish to have? What are the changes you aim to make?

_____

_____

_____

How have you begun to declare those things? Earlier in this book, we highlighted how words reinforce and etch themselves onto our brains. Are your words reinforcing your deep wishes and desires, or are they underlining your fears? In spite of any threats or fears we might have, if we were to consistently train our thoughts to seek out and declare what we hope for and what we expect, then we would begin to condition and prepare ourselves for desired outcomes – regardless of whether they come to pass. It's in the conditioning and the preparation that positive change is taking place.

You **might** get rewarded

You **might** get that job offer

You **might** get supported

Doors **might** open

You **might** fulfill your dreams

You **might** actually succeed.

What is a hope or dream that you have, and have been afraid of visualizing or afraid of declaring out loud? Maybe you might try and write it here... then speak it out loud?

_____

_____

_____

Proverbs 29: 18 – *"Where there is no vision, the people perish..."*

VII.   Keep Trying... Never Give Up.

Change, even when necessary, is usually difficult. Just ask those individuals who make then break resolutions to change only a few weeks into the New Year.

Whenever people attempt to change, we can expect to see a relapse to old patterns of behavior, even if the old pattern is undesirable and even after experiencing the negative consequence of that old behavior. We see this sort of tendency among people who try repeatedly to remain sober or stay out of prison. We also see it among people who repeatedly try to cut back on sweets, have healthy sleep hygiene, lose their temper less, or change their language to life-giving words. Many people sometimes give up on change goals when they fall back on old behaviors. This is nothing new. The Apostle Paul stated how difficult it was for him to do the very thing he wants to do, and the thing he actually does is the very thing he hates (Romans 7:15).

It should therefore come as no surprise when we are trying to change our language and improve our lives that we naturally fall into old behavior patterns. This brings me to my experience with Ava. Ava and I were among a group of people who went to the Dead Sea in Israel. This was the second time for both of us together, however, even as we approached the sea, Ava had begun saying she was not sure she would go in the water. She was making it quite clear that she could not swim and insisted that she would not be able to float in the water. Never mind that the whole time at the Dead Sea, we were reminded that humans can only float on the Dead Sea. Never mind that this situation was playing out almost verbatim as it did some four years earlier, with both Ava and me.

Four years earlier, she had been afraid of floating in that body of water and had stated emphatically and repeatedly that she could not swim. At that time, we had held onto each other until Ava was comfortable enough to recognize she was floating and would not sink. Four years ago, we had both experienced the joy of my friend floating in water for the first time ever. At that time, I had watched her transformation as she pivoted from, "I can't do this!" to, "okay, I'll try" and as she allowed herself to float in water, unassisted, we witnessed a miracle. The miracle of course, was not of her floating. Anyone is able to float in the Dead Sea due to the density of salt in the water. The miracle was actually watching a normally adventurous woman, in spite of her fear, change her internal narrative and become willing to try to do the very thing she had initially been afraid of doing. We had taken pictures of her floating. We had cried with joy. *"No one is going to believe this"*, she had said, between tears of wonder and amazement.

Now, four years later, when I realized we were repeating the same narrative, it was precisely a sense of déjà vu. Why was this happening? Why had my friend lost her confidence? Hadn't she done this very thing before?

Fear is such a liar!

"I can't do this", she faltered.

"You have done this before," I tried to sound assertive. *"You can do it again"*.

However, regardless of how ambivalent she might have tried to sound, Ava had begun walking toward the water. She had started to change her words of doubt, to declaring words of faith and encouragement that she would accomplish this desire to float again in the Dead Sea. I listened to this amazing woman whisper to herself, *"I can do all things through Christ who gives me strength"*. I watched her strides become more confident as she walked toward her goal.

This time, it took her a much shorter time to lay on her back and float, unassisted in the water.

This experience helped me realize that when we make a change once or twice in our lives, it might not be enough to form a habit. People do, in fact fall back to old fears and old ways if they don't practice, practice, practice.

Ava showed me that although she appeared to waiver for a moment, she had a greater will to push against the thoughts that were feeding her fear. She would not give up, so she tried until she found the words, the promises of God, and the language of her faith that would guide her forward.

The experience with Ava was a powerful learning moment for both of us. Ava later told me the act of floating in the Dead Sea represented a new phase in her life and symbolized changes she was ready to make in other areas of her life. For me, this experience humanized the change experience as one that is rife with setbacks and the need to try again and again, until it sticks.

What can you take away from Ava's story that may help you on your own change journey?

_____

_____

_____

Proverbs 24: 16 *"For a just man falleth seven times, and riseth up again..."*

Chapter 12
God's Promises

"Whereby are given unto us exceeding great and precious promises: that by these ye might be partakers of the divine nature...." 2Peter 1:4

By now you are realizing that it is the mindset with which you view experiences that will determine how you interpret and get through those experiences. You may also be realizing that the mindset with which you approach your goals goes a far way in determining whether you will achieve or jeopardize your chances of accomplishing those goals. While a positive mindset might not ensure we get all the outcomes we desire, it certainly builds our resilience and our capacity to deal with issues that arise.

This book offers a guide for positively transforming our lives with the words we use. Throughout this book, I have shared true stories of real people who learned to change their words by reframing their thoughts and beliefs, and in so doing, changed their lives and improved the way they lived. When faced with obstacles or roadblocks and other challenges, it can become difficult to find new words. Thus the need for making the decision and setting the intention to speak productive words and using our courage to follow through.

From many of the stories that are told, whether King David's, Bishop Bonaparte's, Joy's, Elise's, Lisa's, Ava's and so many others, we see how individuals learned to draw on the promises of God. They came to learn that doubt and fear are in direct contradiction with God's plan for their life. After all, doubt and fear are not aligned with the wholeness that God wants for each of us. When we are tempted to fall into the pattern of believing lies about ourselves, we need to remind ourselves, boldly, of God's promises.

God's Word chronicles His promises to us in very clear ways. They are promises to protect us, to provide for our needs, to fight for us, to comfort us, to guide us, to help us, to deliver us from harm, to never leave us, to follow us with goodness and mercy, and many other assurances. If we know the promises of God, and if we memorize and meditate on these promises, we will be etching these words in our mind, and we will be refreshing our wellspring of words, so that these promises become the default narrative to which we automatically turn.

The Bible is the ultimate source for God's promises, and God is faithful to fulfill them all. As we read some of the verses below that are related to the promises of God, it would be beneficial for us to speak them over our life and claim the promises for ourselves.

I have included below, some of my favorite promises of God and I have provided a few examples of how I speak those promises over myself. I believe you will see my pattern and I will leave room for you to speak some of God's promises over yourself.

God's promise: "For God hath not given us the spirit of fear; but of power, and of love, and of a sound mind." (2 Timothy 1:7).

I say: *"God, you have not given me fear, so I will not be afraid. You God, gave me power, love, and a sound mind."*

God's promise: "For the Lord your God is He that goeth with you, to fight for you against your enemies, to save you." (Deuteronomy 20:4).

I say: *"God, your Word says you will be with me and fight for me against my enemies and save me."*

God's promise: "Fear not for I am with you. Do not be dismayed for I am thy God; I will strengthen you. I will help you, yes, I will uphold you with the right hand of my righteousness." (Isaiah 41:10).

I say, *"God, you told me not to be afraid or worried because you will strengthen me, you will help me, and you will even hold me with your right hand of righteousness."*

Now, I invite you to give this a try and use your own words to speak God's promise:

God's promise: "Have I not commanded you? Be strong and courageous. Do not be afraid; do not be discouraged, for the Lord your God will be with you wherever you go." (Joshua 1: 9).

I say _____

_____

_____

God's promise: "He gives power to the faint; and to them that have no might he increaseth strength." (Isaiah 40:29).

I say _____

_____

_____

God's promise: "Therefore I tell you, whatever you ask for in prayer, believe that you have received it and it will be yours." (Mark 11:24).

I say _____

_____

_____

God's promise: "No weapon that is formed against you shall prosper..." (Isaiah 54:17).

I say _____

_____

_____

God's promise: "Though the mountains be shaken and the hills be removed, yet my unfailing love for you will not be shaken nor my covenant of peace be removed," says the Lord, who has compassion on you." (Isaiah 54:10).

I say _____

_____

_____

God's promise: "When you pass through the waters, I will be with you; and when you pass through the rivers, they will not sweep over you. When you walk through the fire, you will not be burned; the flames will not set you ablaze." (Isaiah 43:2 ESV).

I say _____

_____

_____

God's promise: "Do not be anxious about anything, but in every situation, by prayer and petition, with thanksgiving, present your requests to God. And the peace of God, which transcends all understanding, will guard your hearts and your minds in Christ Jesus." (Philippians 4: 6-7 NIV).

I say _____

_____

_____

God's promise: "Fear thou not; for I am with thee: be not dismayed; for I am thy God: I will strengthen thee; yea, I will help thee; yea, I will uphold thee with the right hand of my righteousness." (Isaiah 41:10).

I say _____

_____

_____

God's promise: "Fear not, little flock; for it is your Father's good pleasure to give you the kingdom." (Luke 12: 32).

I say _____

_____

_____

God's promise: "For God so loved the world, that he gave his only begotten Son, that whosoever believeth in him should not perish, but have everlasting life." (John 3:16).

I say _____

_____

_____

Our Heavenly Father is our banner and protector who will guide us and fight for us. I hope this reminder is helpful when you find yourself susceptible to the language of fear and doubt or slipping fast into a chasm of hopelessness. You may put God to the test and take Him at His word.

Chapter 13

Hope

"Hope deferred maketh the heart sick: but when desire cometh, it is a tree of life."
Proverbs 13:12

When we have hope, we believe in possibility, and we can have more of life. More specifically, we have optimism or expectations about good things happening in the near future, when we have hope. When we expect bad things, we feel dread and we are afraid or anxious, however, hope builds within us a capacity to imagine and to believe in the likelihood that positive things can happen to us and for us. Hope is not merely a feel-good emotion. It comprises of thoughts, plans and the will to a bright outcome.

When we have hope, other traits like courage, cheer, energy, optimism, curiosity, and motivation begin to emerge. In every area of life, we come to realize that there is no life without hope. Without hope, an individual can become sick, depressed, and possibly die.

The scriptures point out in Proverbs 13:12 that "Hope deferred maketh the heart sick", this sickness can lead to despair, no wish to live, leading to death of the spirit, and eventually death of the body. The verse continues, "but when the desire cometh, it is a tree of life". This suggests, when we start to wish, when we start to hope, when we start to dream, to envision, to expect, to look forward, or to anticipate; we begin to grow and bear fruit, and we begin to give life to ideas, dreams, and possibilities. Life extends and we eventually learn to function again. In short, it seems difficult to conceive of a life without hope.

I am choosing to share my personal experience with the transformative power of hope and its ability to repair and renew a broken spirit. This life event occurred many years ago, and it sometimes feels like it happened only yesterday. However, it was after I chose hope, that my personal language changed, and my healing began.

It is important that I emphasize again, that while the effort of changing one's language is imperative for living a premier life, it is by no means an easy task. Additionally, we sometimes face situations that can threaten to cripple us and tempt us to revert to old behaviors that produce anger, isolation, hurt, shame or other feelings that will deter us from living an abundant life. Against that backdrop, here is my story of a time I came to choose hope.

My husband and I had separated more than two months earlier; and I was devastated, scared, hurt, angry, and very, very heartbroken. This was not the life I had envisioned for myself, and I also believed this was not the life he had envisioned. I really did not understand how both of us had gotten to this point of separation, yet, I remained hopeful that we would figure things out and restore our relationship to better than it was before.

One morning, in one of our rare communications, he called to tell me his good friend had died in his arms. I at once imagined the trauma, the shock, and the sadness he probably experienced. In that moment, I forgot about the man I thought had caused me hurt, and only remembered the best-friend and the love who I had known and married. My thoughts immediately turned from anger and hurt to, concern and great care. *"How is he doing? How is he coping? How is he holding it together?"* I wondered silently. I could not help thinking that he must have been hurting so deeply and I tried to imagine how I might help him, while also wondering whether he would accept my support. *"Go. Don't go."* My thoughts warred inside, so I prayed for wisdom, pushed against all my fears and decided to support him by attending the funeral. My husband and I had been each other's person before and so I made the decision to support him in his grief.

The heaviness that I felt as I drove to that funeral, did not match the surprisingly, mild temperature of that Autumn Saturday. I tried looking for signs that things would be okay, and I kept asking God to keep everything in order. When I arrived at the Church, the husband I had conjured in my mind, who would welcome my presence, was not the person I saw. Instead, the man I saw appeared distant. His voice lacked warmth and his eyes seemed empty toward me. Was it disdain toward me? Maybe it was grief, or maybe it was shock. Maybe it was all of those emotions wrapped together. Yet in my mind, it seemed that my presence at that funeral had been quite a mistake.

At the graveside, I tried to blame my trembling nerves on the afternoon chill. I searched for calm in the changing colors of leaves on the trees, but I could not ignore the irony that my husband and I were standing directly across from each other, with a gaping hole in the ground between us. The loss of a loved one is likened to a savage tearing of the flesh and even as the coffin lowered into this hole, it was hard to distinguish which loss was worse. Even then I wondered again, how had our relationship come to this bleak moment?

After the burial, I got in my car and drove from that cemetery alone, not knowing what to do as the cold numb of despair began to spread like a chill through me. *"Where are you God?"* I cried out in my car. I waited, I listened, and hearing silence, I wept silently. *"God, this pain really hurts. Why are you keeping me alive? Please, please show me your purpose. This pain could not be the reason, for which I was born, could it?"* My soul ached as I tried to push away the tightness in my chest.

The following day was Sunday, and against every natural power, I went to Church. If I took slow, deep breaths, I could probably hold back the tears that were flooding my eyes. That morning, I could neither look at nor speak to anyone, so I remained silent and avoided all eye contact. The sermon I heard, (which may not have been the one everyone else heard), came from the scripture, Hebrews 11:1. It states in part, "Now, faith is the substance of things hoped for..." The question I heard the Lord God ask me quite plainly was, *"What do you want, Denise? What is it you hope for?"* The question was directed at me, it was clear, and it made me pause and ask myself, *"What did I hope for? What did I want?"*

When you are halted in your thoughts like I was, and obliged to make a choice, well you choose. My response to the question *"What do you want? What do you hope for?"* was that I wanted to live. As much as I had felt the previous day like my life was slipping away, on this Sunday, I wanted to live. I wanted to write books. I wanted to change lives for the better. I wanted a healthy, loving relationship. I wanted my marriage to be healed and restored. It was here I learned I had to speak the life-giving words of hope to myself. I wanted to use my talents to honor God. I wanted to live the best version of the life God had given me.

Just whispering those words softly to myself at first, turned on a glimmer of a new light within me. Almost immediately, I felt my despair begin to lessen at the prompt of those five words, *"What do you hope for?"* and my response, *"I want to live!"*. I remember leaving Church that day completely changed from the way I had arrived. After I left Church, I sang out loud in my car, I met my sister and we went for a walk. We talked about future hopes and dreams, and I was looking forward to possibilities ahead. That afternoon, I had chosen hope.

The inactive mind naturally thinks of all the things that can go bad, and our default is to speak of things with a negative slant. However, it is important to try and speak with hope.

Developing a language of faith is also a certain way of cultivating hope. Hope makes us want to live. Hope makes us want to go on. I was also learning that hope can bloom with even a tiny amount of faith.

With that tiny amount of faith, I adjusted my thoughts to focus on my hopes and what lie ahead. I acknowledged the life I still had and realized I wanted to live it victoriously. I told myself that God would not have brought me through all the difficulties I had survived, to have that moment be my final moment. I declared that was not how my story would end. I reminded myself that God wants the best for me. I started to remember and repeat the promises of God, that He loves me. My heavenly Daddy loves me.

Sometimes we need to change our focus and shift our position, to get a turnaround in our lives.

Sometimes it is necessary to cling to hope in order to obtain a breakthrough.

Eventually, I got most of the things I hoped for on that Sunday. However, by drawing on a language of hope, I had begun to condition myself to thrive and to withstand the challenges that were to come. I had begun the turnaround that was needed to achieve the things I had hoped for. That Sunday morning, I had entered the church feeling like my spirit was on life support, and with just one prompt, *"What do you hope for?"* I felt the nudge that was needed to change my focus, shift my mindset, tap into a willingness to choose hope, latch onto thoughts of what was possible, and therefore I was able to begin my own personal healing.

I share this story knowing that if this turnaround is possible for me, the same is also possible for you. I believe that God did this for me, by changing the words I used in my situation, and He can do the same for you.

Chapter 14

There is Power in your "I am…"

"For I know the thoughts I think toward you, saith the LORD, thoughts of peace, and not of evil, to give you an expected end." Jeremiah 29:11

Many of us are ardently trying to find out who we are. There are times we become attached to identities that lead us to describe ourselves as deficits and what we are not, when we should be describing ourselves the way God sees us. God created us and saw that His creation was good, so let us remind ourselves, who God says we are.

So many times, we create a narrative that contradicts the way God sees us. The enemy whispers in our ear or uses circumstances to tell us that we will never be qualified, worthy, or adequate. Sometimes people, who should have been pouring good words in us, instead tell us that we are not good enough, and we fall into the trap of believing those lies. When God tells us that we are wonderfully made (Psalm 139:14), we believe we are deficient. When God says we are the light of the world (Matthew 5:14), we believe we are invisible. When God tells us that we are as essential as salt (Matthew 5:13), we believe we are ordinary and unimportant.

We attach to words that contradict who God says we are, then we repeat those words, over and over, until eventually we believe them and even worse, others believe them too. We believe the hurtful, painful lies, and they wear us down until we no longer remember or believe who God says we are.

As seeds of doubt begin to take root; shame and insecurity begin to grow. On the outside, we may smile and appear to be doing well, yet behind our smiles and in the back of our minds are whispers that we are not enough. What was it that caused that hurt? What led you to believe those lies? I urge you to turn and cling instead to words of life and hope; and repeat who God says you are.

We have the capacity to code in our brains the ideas we are willing to believe about ourselves and the limits of what we believe is possible. We can revise the code or completely revamp it, when it no longer is working for us and when it no longer is directing us to our goals.

In other words, you have the power to choose your thoughts. When you decide to change your thoughts about yourself, change the stories you tell yourself, and repeat them until you believe them. In doing so, you will be giving your brain a new code or set of instructions from which to operate. It is then that you will begin to see a new change in how you experience your life. This also means that if you change the way you think about your circumstance, you can come to see your circumstance change.

Developing a new story takes practice. The mind needs preparation, conditioning, renewing, and training in order to open itself to be willing to develop a new story with new words. Muhammad Ali kept repeating, "I am the greatest," until his mind accepted this was so. What is your "I am…?" Just as there are power in your words, there is great power in your "I am…" I suggest we begin with reminding ourselves of who we are and who God says we are.

Why do we give in to the lies that people or circumstances tell us, when God sees us in the best light and His Word tells us who we are? God calls us redeemed, so I will say, "I am redeemed." God calls us fearfully made, so I will say, "I am fearfully made." God says we are blessed, so we may say, "I am blessed." The appalling circumstances of her life could have led Elise to continue claiming a defeated, "I am…" Instead, as she came to learn that God called her favored, she practiced saying, "I am favored." She came to learn that God loved her, so she learned to say, "I am loved." When she remembered God had given her power, she came to say, "I am a woman with power." I am thankful that Lisa eventually untangled herself from her professor's words, and began telling herself, "I am talented," "I am gifted," "I am a writer." I am inspired by the way Ava encouraged herself and committed to keep trying even though trying felt scary.

We can reinforce this new way of talking to ourselves when we acknowledge our own strengths as well as the way God sees us. Changing this view of ourselves will not happen overnight, but the more we rehearse our "I am..." the more our brains will embrace this new identity that is showered in kindness and mirrors who God says we are. We must say this new "I am..." over and over, because each time we do so, we are strengthening the habit of uplifting ourselves, building up ourselves, and restoring ourselves, until we can see in ourselves, the good workmanship that God created.

The following pages will guide you as you aim to develop your own positive image of your "I am..."

To get started, I encourage you to make a list of your strengths. If you are having difficulty coming up with any strengths, just ask others you trust, who know you well. You may ask two or three coworkers, family members, or friends, *"What do you see as my strengths?"* Then write them down and start making a list. I started a list, which you may continue or modify.

I am smart

I am brave

I am a loyal friend

I am creative

I am happy

I am...

I am…

Notice the list consists only of words that uplift the spirit. Below, I have also included some of the things that God's Word says about us.

I am blessed (Genesis 1:27 – 28; Galatians 3:14)

I am victorious (1 Corinthians 15:57)

I am more than a conqueror (Romans 8:37)

I am courageous (Joshua 1:9)

I am light (Matthew 5:14)

I am fearfully and wonderfully made (Psalms 139:14)

I am chosen (John 15:16; 1Peter 2:9)

I am redeemed (Ephesians 1:7)

I am restored (Joel 2:25)

I am healed (Isaiah 53:5)

I am delivered (Isaiah 41:10)

I am powerful (2 Timothy 1:7)

I am a child of God (1John 3:1; Romans 8:16)

I am strong (Deuteronomy 31:6, Joshua 1:9)

I am beautifully made (Ecclesiastes 3:11)

I am valued (Jeremiah 29:11)

I am loved (John 3:16)

I am forgiven (Ephesians 1:7; 1 John 1:9)

I am....

I am....

I am....

I am....

Once you start building your list, you may notice it getting longer, and you are preparing for the next step of this activity. Creating your own, "I am..." with the help of a sun image. I use the sun which represents a bright, positive, larger than life image to reinforce the brightness and the energy that will begin to nourish and nurture some new language for your minds. At the center of the image are the words, "I am..." because there is tremendous power in our "I am...".

Below is an example of one person's "I am..."

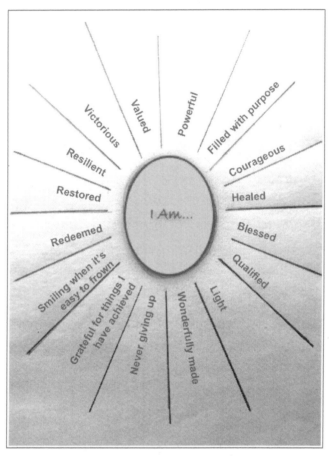

Now take your time and create your own affirmations about yourself. Since this is a new habit, you get to practice each day, to really look at your sun image and repeat, out loud, the strengths you possess. Boldly. Confidently. As though you believe it. I AM Beautiful! I AM Blessed! I AM Talented! I AM Smart!

I have included a blank sun image on the following page, for you to begin identifying and declaring your own strengths. Some people place a picture of themselves in the center, so you may be as creative as you wish.

Include who you are, and who God says you are. Remember, it is what we rehearse in our minds that we will eventually come to believe, and it is what we believe, we will come to achieve.

There is power in your "I am...," just take a look at the things you believe about yourself that are not true or not uplifting. These things did not get planted yesterday. They have been germinating, and growing and taking root, for days, months, even years. It will take time to replace those lies with the powerful truths that God wants you to know.

Remember there is power in your "I am...". So now I urge you to commit to affirming the "I am..." that will help you on your journey as you pivot toward becoming the best version of your life that your heavenly Father intended for you.

Chapter 15

Sing a New Song

"O sing unto the Lord a new song; for he hath done marvelous things: his right hand, and his holy arm, hath gotten him the victory." Psalm 98:1

Songs of hope offer a way to reinforce words of life into our brain. Music stimulates and restores our brain and helps to renew our minds in remarkable ways. Music with words can make a message more appealing and more memorable. On the following pages I have shared titles of some songs that I play regularly, and sing, dance, or otherwise enjoy, in order to reinforce a wellspring of words, a language of life, health to my bones, and cleansing of my mind to honor this temple. What are some songs or music that you can use?

Speak Life by Toby Mac
God's not done with you by Tauren Wells
Fight Song by Rachel Platten
Rise Up by Andra Day
You Say by Lauren Daigle
The Break up Song by Francesca Battistelli
Look up Child by Lauren Daigle
I'm Trading my Sickness by Darrell Evans
Move (Keep Walking) Toby Mac
I'm Alive by Michael Franti

I Smile by Kirk Franklin

Unwritten by Natasha Beddingfield

Superwoman by Alicia Keys

This Girl is on Fire by Alicia Keys

Conqueror by Estelle

Walking on Water by Need to Breathe

Part the Waters by Evie

We Fall Down by Donnie McClurkin

Thrive by Casting Crowns

Praise Him in Advance by Marvin Sapp

Overcomer by Mandisa

Every Praise by Hezekiah Walker

I Believe (Island Medley) by Jonathan Nelson

Here, I invite you to make your own list:

Chapter 16

Finale

"Give ear to my words, O LORD, consider my meditation." Psalm 5:1

Almost from the first moment I became aware of the power of words, I started to learn and understand how psychology and the sciences reinforced or incorporated that same premise. People from all over the world, who teach, influence, persuade, counsel, challenge, convert, and in other ways communicate; do so by leveraging the power and nuance of words.

My personal journey of change was a commitment that I made to be better, after I had witnessed change in others and after some experiences that made me want more for myself. However, it is the instructions in these pages, along with my faith, and my growing relationship with God that continue to guide me as I improve my language and my own narrative.

You too are welcome to a relationship with God. All you need to do is to repeat this prayer, "Dear God, I believe you are God. Please forgive my sins and come into my heart. Change my heart today I pray, in Jesus' name. Amen." If you repeated this prayer and meant it with sincerity, I believe you have entered into relationship with God and He has accepted you as His own. Please locate a Bible-based Church so you may grow in your relationship with God, increase your faith, and so you may learn to walk confidently in the knowledge of how God sees you.

My own journey is ongoing. May the wellspring from which you draw your speech, your language, your thoughts, and your daily words, be refreshed and renewed so you may live an abundant life of hope, energy, and kindness. I believe that this is the life we were all intended to live.

A Charge

No more through this reality will I drift
To truly live, I must rewrite the script.
Time is long but life is short.

My personal script is a paradigm shift
To transcend the mundane with a spiritual lift.

Blindness is caused by illusion,
So, I will close the rift
That separates us from the One
Who in the first place gave us the Gift.

Ian R. Shaw ©2012

Works Cited

1. Leaf, Caroline. *Switch on Your Brain: The Key to Peak Happiness, Thinking, and Health*. Baker Books, 2013.

2. Fuchs, Eberhard, & Gabriele Flügge. "Adult neuroplasticity: more than 40 years of research." *Neural plasticity* vol. 2014 541870. 4 May, 2014, doi:10.1155/2014/541870.

3. Shaffer, Joyce. "Neuroplasticity and Clinical Practice: Building Brain Power for Health." *Frontiers in psychology* vol. 7 1118. 26 Jul. 2016, doi:10.3389/fpsyg.2016.01118.

4. *Brain basics: Understanding sleep. National Institute of Neurological Disorders and Stroke.* https://www.ninds.nih.gov/Disorders/Patient-Caregiver-Education/Understanding-Sleep. Accessed 13 May, 2019.

5. Newberg, Andrew B. and Mark Robert Waldman. *Words Can Change Your Brain: 12 Conversation Strategies to Build Trust, Resolve Conflict, and Increase Intimacy.* Avery, 2012.

6. *The Nobel Prize in Physiology or Medicine 1981.* www.nobelprize.org/nobel_prizes/medicine/laureates/1981/. Accessed 31 Oct. 2014.

7. Rockefeller, K. *Visualize confidence: How to use guided imagery to overcome self-doubt.* New Harbinger Publications, 2007.

8. "How Sports Became Us." Freakonomics Radio. NPR, New York. 12 Sep. 2018. Radio.

9. Day, S. *Theory and Design in Counseling and Psychotherapy.* 2nd Edition. Brooks/Cole, 2008.

10. *Life is Beautiful.* Directed by Roberto Benigni, Miramax Home Entertainment, 1999.

11. Hendry, Erica. "7 Epic Fails Brought to you by the Genius Mind of Thomas Edison." *Smithsonian Magazine, 20 Nov. 2013,* https://www.smithsonianmag.com/innovation/7-epic-fails-brought-to-you-by-the-genius-mind-of-thomas-edison-180947786/ Accessed 20 May, 2019.

12. "I Am Still the Greatest", *This I Believe.* NPR, New York. 6 Apr. 2009. Radio.

13. Velin, Bob. "Muhammad Ali's legendary career." *USA Today Sports.* 4 Jun. 2016. https://www.usatoday.com/story/sports/2016/06/04/muhammad-ali-fight-by-fight-career/85341622/ Accessed 14 Oct. 2018.

Acknowledgements

I thank God for the words on these pages. Almost 13 years ago, the seeds of this work began to sprout, then after I re-read Rick Warren's *Purpose Driven Life,* this book began to take shape. This journey happened in the company of some prominent men and women, to whom I am thankful for their words of encouragement, enthusiasm, and prayers.

My remarkable family, Donna, Naydene, Mark, Annette, Peter, and Raakhi, you listened, encouraged, reframed, nudged, and encouraged again. Adrienne, Alexandra, Arielle, and Ashley, your artistic talents, insight, and inspiration are gifts. Please continue to use your talents without apology and let your light shine brilliantly.

Dr. Wayne and Mrs. Monica Solomon you have worked tirelessly and patiently to encourage and help me produce a caliber product.

Some of the forever people in my life like Violet Vernon, Sandra Volel, Karen Thompson, and Keith A. Robb, I thank God for placing you in my life to dream this dream with me. Dr. Lisa Brooks-Greaux, Michele Phillips, and Pierre Dobson, we call ourselves "The Village" and I am thankful that we feed each other with life-giving words and remind each other that like eagles, we are made to soar.

Gavin Simpson, Alex Lee, Ian and Cheryl Shaw, and my SoKA writing group Carol, Janet, and Kathy, thank you for your ears, your insight, your feedback, your words, your stories, and your gentle prodding from so long ago.

Bishop Philip Bonaparte, your prayers and words of prophecy held me to the course. Karen Clark, your messages offered a daily dose of encouragement. Bishop Donald Hilliard, Jr., you were the first person I heard say, "speak those things which aren't as though they are." I have an army of prayer warriors; however, Sonia Allen, Gail Burgess, Hannah Pratt, and Gilo Admaya Thomas, your wisdom, your laughter, and your unceasing prayers have been essential ingredients in this project.

Tracy Fox Galluppi, you've been a foot soldier on this journey with me. I thank you with all my heart.

Cynthia Forrester, God in His infinite wisdom, knew I would need your guidance after my own mother would no longer be here, so He selected you to be my godmother. You perform this role excellently. From the start, you understood, encouraged, and believed in this project. I am thankful for your words and your love.

To the persons whose stories helped bring this work to life: you are courageous, you are resilient, and I believe your stories have already begun to transform lives. To all who read this book and to whomever you speak, I hope you use your words to speak with kindness; and when you speak, leave others with their dignity intact.

Endorsements

Many books are about theory, wishful thinking, or ideas that sound good, but have very little to do with the actual lives we live. But not this book! Dr. Denise Williams, who was a member of a top global consulting firm, writes in "**Wellspring of Words**" ideas that come from experience and are supported by both scripture and science.

Denise uses multiple sources and examples, including relevant stories and testimonies, to show how these ideas transformed not just others, but her own mental models as well (neuronal plasticity). "**Wellspring of Words**" is easy to read, structured, and inspires one to believe in oneself and others. I can't wait to read the published copy!

Fred Garmon, PhD. LeaderLabs, Inc.

=======================================

I've just turned the final page of Dr. Denise Williams' **Wellspring of Words** and am filled with gratitude for her and the words, stories, and encouragement she's woven together for humanity. Elegantly blending brain science, optimism research, and spirituality, she's created a gentle yet very powerful guide for developing a mindset to support achieving and living in one's personal greatness. **Wellspring** is a guide, how-to, and devotional all wrapped into one compelling and super readable book that deserves a place on your bookshelf today!

Carol Camerino, Multi-certified Career Coach, Professional Resume Writer, and Author of Words for the Journey www.LookingfortheOnRamp.com and www. RestartingYourCareerAcademy. com

At last, an in-depth exploration into understanding why words, whether spoken or unspoken, have so much power to change lives. *Wellspring of Words* is a masterfully written, easy-to-follow guide for anyone who wants to experience the rejuvenating and transformative effects of a positive narrative and an optimistic mindset. This magnificent book offers a compelling and inspiring reminder of who God says we are; and Dr. Denise Williams is a story-teller who weaves in the courage and vulnerabilities of extraordinary people to highlight the powerful impact of the words we use. It is not often that we find a book that bundles together scientific and biblical insights to offer practical **DAILY** applications. So, for every person who wants to make lasting, personal improvements, *Wellspring of Words* is a must-have and a definite, must-read.

Philip M. Bonaparte, MD., is a Senior Pastor, Medical Doctor, and co-author of *Forgiveness from the Heart.*

=======================================

As Director of a national organization that brings life-changing opportunities to people, I am thrilled to find a book that provides the same. *Wellspring of Words* offers a formula for changing our relationship with our words. I believe every person will read then re-read with pen in hand to capture and engage with the gems in this book. Dr. Denise Williams is witty, her language lyrical, and I strongly recommend her book as a resource for shifting mindsets, building resilience, connecting with our faith, and speaking words of hope.

Stacey-Ann Easy: Director of Garden of Dreams Foundation; Board Member of Make-A-Wish New Jersey; and Emmy award winner for MSG Classroom.

173

Made in the USA
Middletown, DE
09 February 2022

60855963R00099